The
ARMS
RACE

The ARMS RACE

Baseball's Thought Leaders Share Their
Secrets to Pitching Development

COACH RON WOLFORTH

The Arms Race: Baseball's Thought Leaders Share Their Secrets to Pitching Development

BMD Publishing
All Rights Reserved

ISBN # 978-1705561072

BMDPublishing@MarketDominationLLC.com
MarketDominationLLC.com

BMD Publishing CEO: Seth Greene
Editorial Management: Bruce Corris
Technical Editor & Layout: Kristin Watt

Printed in the United States of America.

ACKNOWLEDGMENTS

First to my wife Jill, my daughter Samantha, and my son Garrett: You three are the epicenter of my universe. You make me incredibly proud every single day of my life. I not only do this for you, but I'm able to do what I do every day only through your unwavering love and support.

To my staff: Each one of you is amazing and inspirational in your own way. You make me better. It is an honor and a privilege to work with you and next to you every day.

To all those who contributed to these chapters: You guys are inspirations to me and thousands of others in the baseball universe. In the poem of baseball development, each of you has contributed your own unique verse. Thank you for your support in this endeavor. It means more than you could ever know.

To Bruce Corris and Kristin Watt: I am grateful for your assistance and efforts with the interviews and the editing. Your contributions were simply invaluable.

And finally, thank you to all who doubted, discounted and disparaged me along my personal journey. Your negativity, arrogance and pessimism fueled my fire to continually overcome your cynicism and defeatism, and aided in my efforts to try to make the world a more hopeful and inspiring place.

INTRODUCTION

One of my college professors in graduate school described me to our class at large as an esoteric, eclectic learner. I will admit, at the time I wasn't entirely sure from what context his description was coming, and if his characterization of me was actually a compliment or a criticism. I literally rushed back to my dorm and feverishly reviewed my understanding of the words. After 15 minutes of research and contemplation, while I thought his description was both very insightful and accurate, I was no closer in deciding if it was an accolade or a disparagement.

That was 1984.

Today, over 25 years later, I remain an esoteric, eclectic learner, and I also remain unsure if my learning style is a good thing or not. However, I have come to the realization that this is indeed the best way for me personally to process information and connect the dots.

Which leads me to the thought process behind this book.

A dear long-time coaching friend of mine is Gary Hatch of Bellingham, Washington. He commonly closes his correspondences to me with a catchy little phrase: "*All of Us* Is Better Than *Any One of Us!*"

I wholeheartedly agree.

With both those insights in mind, I made a list of the most forward-thinking baseball people I know. I sought out people who challenge the status quo and rail against "group think" and traditional hyperbole. I sought out people who really had something of merit and significance to offer to the baseball and pitching communities.

This group is made up of not only men that I admire and respect, but men I have personally known for many years. They are close friends and confidants. All of them are life-long learners. All of them are open, curious, and driven to grow and discover.

So here I am again, drawing insight and inspiration from multiple sources and perspectives. It is my hope that this book will, at the very least, expand your current understanding of pitching a baseball and the development of the competitive pitching athlete. These men have made a real difference in my life, and I hope I've made a difference in theirs.

As Coach Hatch routinely says, "All of us is better than any one of us."

Welcome to being challenged and pushed.

Welcome to, as the late great Ken Ravizza said, "Being comfortable being uncomfortable!"

Welcome to the revolution, and thinking differently.

Welcome to *The Arms Race.*

Coach Ron Wolforth
February 2020

TABLE OF CONTENTS

CHAPTER 1

THE RON WOLFORTH STORY

If you haven't read one of my previous books, or been to the Texas Baseball Ranch®, you may be wondering, just who is Ron Wolforth? Why did I decide to do this book? How was I able to get all these Major League coaches and cutting edge thought leaders to be interviewed? And how did the Texas Baseball Ranch become one of the country's best-known and respected training facilities for pitchers in the world today?

Let's start at the beginning: Me as a player.

One of the more common questions I get is regarding my playing career. Was I a good college pitcher? Did I pitch professionally?

In truth, in every way a post high school career can be measured, my college career sat somewhere between incredibly underwhelming to non existent. This fact is very important because this abject failure during this period of my life was the very impetus for me becoming who and what I am today.

Growing up I was routinely told that if I wanted something bad enough, I could achieve it. All I had to do was commit to the goal and work my tail off and it would happen.

Well, no 18-22 year old in the United States wanted to play baseball professionally more than I did. I was "ALL in" toward my goal! I was very coachable. I was a good student. I had a very good arm. I was a good athlete.

Why then, if I was all of these things, were my results between the ages of 18-22 so substandard?

That very question has lingered and burned inside of me for the last 35+ years.

One of the driving forces in my life and my business has been to help as many young men with similar talents, drives and ambitions as I had at 18 make real positive strides toward their dreams instead of having them detoured, diverted, diluted or squashed.

At my company, Texas Baseball Ranch, we state that the primary mission of our organization is to help a young athlete play one level higher than they otherwise would have without our assistance and mentoring. Critics would point out that this goal is unprovable. How could we possibly know if we achieved our goal?

In my opinion, those asking that question often miss an absolutely critical point of the mission statement itself. So much of success lies in the mindset of the performer.

The challenge is to first define for each athlete what the exact skills and abilities required to play at that next level are and work diligently and purposely toward improving and enhancing those skills and abilities. Furthermore, our philosophy is to be constantly striving, pushing, reaching and growing and just as importantly to avoid placing artificial, unconscious or arbitrary limits or constraints on an athlete. Just as importantly, we objectively measure and then track our progression.

How has this philosophy worked?

At the time of the writing of this segment:

423 of our athletes have exceeded the 90 mph barrier
142 of our athletes have topped the 94 mph mark
22 of our athletes have broken 100 mph
121 of our athletes have been drafted

So in short, this philosophy has worked incredibly well.

We never tell any athlete what goal is reachable or attainable and which ones are not. Instead we view it as our daily objective to paint a very clear and concise picture of the incremental steps he needs to take today to move 1% closer toward that goal. We know that if the athlete can accomplish THAT on a regular basis, he will have an exceptional chance at moving on to the next level of competition.

This is the essence of the Texas Baseball Ranch: To improve .036% today... 25% this week... 1% this month and 12% this year...and if we can do this for 5 consecutive years, magic absolutely happens.

My Coaching Journey

I started out as a baseball graduate assistant at Sam Houston State University. While at first blush that may sound like a great start, it basically meant I tamped the mound, I cut the grass and I cleaned the bathrooms...and those were three of my more important tasks.

Early on into that experience, the head softball coach at Sam Houston State University pulled me aside and said, "What do you think about joining us as a grad assistant?" At the time they had a top 5 ranked Division II softball team. I didn't know much about fastpitch softball, so initially I was very hesitant. But he told me I'd actually be coaching, teaching and traveling with the team. So I said, "Let's give it a try."

I did quite well and I moved up very quickly in the ranks, and just three years later I became the Head Softball Coach at the University of Nebraska. I coached there for six years and went to two College World Series but deep down inside my heart remained with my baseball and pitching roots.

The Transition From Coaching To Training

Our venture into private training began in Canada. My assistant coach at Nebraska, my wife, and I created an academy in Vancouver, British Columbia. It was called the CAN-AM Baseball/Softball Academy. We called it CAN-AM because it was Americans teaching in Canada. We ran that academy very successfully for two years.

My wife Jill and I wanted to get back to Texas, so we moved and opened our first academy in Houston in 1996.

All the while, I was thinking how great it would be if we could create a truly unique training facility with acres of land, state of the art buildings, and most importantly, cutting-edge training programs. A place that would provide holistic, forward-thinking, innovative training that had never been done before. We strived to look at things in a different way and from a much broader perspective. So we saved up our money for multiple years, bought 20 acres of raw property, purchased the small barn for an office and opened the Texas Baseball Ranch in 2006.

We immediately sought to make our training unique in the baseball universe and tapped into a lot of the training processes that had evolved in golf, martial arts, track and field and swimming and applied a 'constraint-led approach' thinking to baseball. We zeroed in on the objective measurement of training, which was not prevalent in baseball at the time. Most other training at the time was compelling a specific choreography, and success was defined by a player's movements 'looking better'...whatever that meant to the eye of the trainer.

Instead, what we did was really try to objectively measure the 'results' of the training, and see if the training did indeed lead to improvements in game-time performance. As you can imagine, the answer was, 'sometimes it did, sometimes it didn't'. The key for us was being able to determine which training segments and applications really did have a positive impact and which did not. So, from there, we started to get better and better as that training became more precise, more reliable and more usable.

At the Beginning…Viewed as Heretics

It's funny, when we began, we were perceived in the baseball world as crazy, heretics, provocateurs….way outside the lines. We were viewed as a kind of a pariah in baseball. But over the years, what we did became more and more mainstream.

Today, 2020, we're really at the center of the new training, technology and process. Elite levels of baseball have paid attention. In the past year for example, more than half of all Major League organizations have visited the Ranch.

Science, logic, reason and research play a large role in what we do at the Texas Baseball Ranch. Of course research remains only a part of what we do because we have come to understand that to be a leader one can't always wait for the research to tell you where to go. Instead we use research to support and reinforce our thoughts, philosophies and processes.

Vern Gambetta, who has long been a pioneer in athletic training, may have said it best, *'If you wait for the research to tell you where to go, you're soon going to be 15-20 years behind the curve. You have to use your intuitive knowledge and experience. Many times you have to go out in front of the research, and then do research to confirm that you're on the right track.'* So our innovation is really a marriage between science and research and our own common sense and instincts.

The most visible proof, of the impact our training was having on pitchers, was increased velocity. In baseball, we've seen a dramatic improvement in throwing velocity for pitchers of all ages and at all levels. While this in part has been very satisfying, as with all innovation, the growth has definitely been uneven. Far too often for our taste, people have co-opted the velocity enhancement portion of the training and have forgotten or underemphasized the supplemental or synergistic elements of arm health/durability, recovery, command, deception and sequencing.

Whenever I address parents I give them an analogy, which really resonates with most of them:

Pitching is FAR more than just trying to win a teddy bear at the carnival by hitting a number on the radar gun.

You are going to have to command it.

You are going to have to spin it.

You are going to have to change speeds with it.

You are going to have to throw it 100+ times and be able to bounce back like it never happened 5 days from now...or throw it 25 times and be able to bounce back tomorrow like tonight never happened.

You are going to have to be pretty much the same pitcher each and every time out. (consistency)

You are going to have to do all of this over a 6 month period.

When people look at pitching, a lot of times they don't see the holism of being a good pitcher. Everyone sees velocity. It's the radar gun that sticks out but there's so much more that is intertwined in becoming an elite pitcher.

It is not difficult to find a guy working at a Home Depot who was able to throw 92 miles per hour in his youth but just couldn't stay healthy and/or perform well enough at the professional level to ascend and his career was fairly short or non existent.

Holism, Integration & Hyper-Personalization

So, at the Texas Baseball Ranch, what we really do is try to understand the holism, the entire equation. This starts with doing a good job of assessing a player.

Let's say an 18-year-old pitcher comes to us. We're going to do six different assessments to try to figure out what could possibly be constraining him from being a top prospect or ascending levels. Is it indeed just velocity? Is it command? Is it secondary pitches like curveball or slider? Does he recover well or have trouble bouncing back? Does he have a problem with health and durability? When you understand what specifically is constraining him, then you can really help him.

There is an essential truth about velocity enhancement that actually surprises most people. We have our coaches boot camp every December where coaches from professional organizations, colleges, high schools and private training centers are in attendance. I try to share this paradigm with them at every event. In my PowerPoint there's a slide that says "Velocity creation, or enhancement, is actually formulaic." And it truly is. There are about a dozen things one can do to enhance velocity and about a half dozen things one can eliminate that will help unleash it. If you take that holistic approach and address all those items simultaneously, you're almost always going to see an improvement in velocity.

Velocity Enhancement is Formulaic

As I mentioned before, velocity creation, in and of itself, is very formulaic once you understand it. Think of it as an equation. However, it's a very involved equation and we often don't know which variable per individual is going to be the most significant. Some people may need to gain strength while for others, strength is not their primary constraint.

Therefore, when you tell every pitcher on your staff, "Let's get in the weight room and get big!", understand that some may make a significant jump because strength is exactly what they needed, but others will see no improvement or may actually go backward because they spent too much time on an area they didn't need to work on.

It all starts with a healthy, durable arm, which entails training the entire body. The primary goal of the human body is to not hurt itself. So it is going to be very resistant in allowing your arm to go as fast as it might. Which means the first step in creating world class velocity is to create a healthy, durable arm and a very flexible, mobile and stable body.

Health and durability is where velocity begins. From there, we can get more and more precise and specific on velocity creation. We're very good at the velocity enhancement part but we also realized several years ago that it's only one piece of the performance puzzle, not the entire puzzle itself.

Along the way, 121 of our young men have been drafted by Major League teams. Some have made it to the major leagues. We believe a number of others are on the cusp, in Double A or Triple A, heading to the big leagues. That's really special. Becoming a professional pitcher is difficult enough, but becoming a Major Leaguer is truly a remarkable accomplishment.

Trevor Bauer is probably our best-known alumnus. He started with us as an eighth grader and improved very rapidly. He still holds the record at the Ranch with a 105.6 mile an hour throw of a regulation baseball.

We're also very proud of our reconstruction efforts, being able to help guys who were struggling, or even out of baseball, get back to the big leagues. Guys like C.J. Wilson, Scottie Kazmir, Barry Zito and Chien-Ming Wang. We've also had a good mixture of young guys moving up, former stars getting rehabbed, and current stars coming to us for augmentation and help such as Justin Verlander, Erik Johnson, Tyson Ross and Bud Norris.

I remember the moment it became clear that we had arrived on Major League Baseball's radar screen. It was when Trevor Bauer was traded from the Arizona Diamondbacks to the Cleveland Indians. I was giving a lecture at the Ranch and I looked up and the Indians' general manager Chris Antonetti and manager Terry Francona were in the front row taking notes. To have a Major League manager and general manager come all the way down to a facility in Montgomery, Texas to hear what we had to say, that was when I said, "Okay, this is the real true testament to what we've built here."

Speaking of the Major Leagues, in this book you're going to get the benefit of a lot of big league experience. Several Major League pitching coaches are going to share their knowledge and their insights. These are guys we've known, been working with and along side for nearly 20 years.

Success Leaves Clues

I remember at one of our very first Ultimate Pitching Coaches Bootcamp, in the first few rows sat Brent Strom, Derek Johnson, and Wes Johnson. At the time, Brent was the Pitching Coordinator for the Washington Nationals, Derek was a coach at Stetson University, and Wes was a high school coach in Arkansas. All three, sitting there taking notes. Now they're all accomplished Major League pitching coaches, and Brent has a World Series ring.

Twenty years ago, no one had any idea we'd be where we are today. But here we are, still collaborating. We've shared together, we've grown together, and we've learned together. I think the collective group has really changed baseball in the way it is taught, and the way it is trained, especially on the pitching end.

Twenty years is a long time. A lot has changed in pitching development during that time. A lot of minds have been changed. How many times has something like this happened? Something new comes out and people think it's a terrible idea. It's absurd. It gets rejected or attacked because it's different than the accepted way. But gradually it becomes accepted, and eventually it's viewed as, "Well, that's the way it's always been."

That's certainly how it's been with us. When we started out with this 'weighted ball stuff', we were viewed as just absolutely dangerous and putting young people at absolute risk. But we took our time, and we used objective measurement to find out the efficacy of how we were proceeding. We started to have success story after success story after success story. Eventually Major League Baseball had to look at this and go, "Their track record's just too good. They're turning out too many high caliber, high quality people, There's something to this."

Looking Forward

But enough looking back. Let's get out the crystal ball and think about what's coming down the road in professional baseball.

What's going to have the biggest impact, particularly on the development of pitchers?

Many will tell you analytics and sabermetrics are really changing the game. While I do believe that is true, I have a slightly different take on how they are utilized. While analytics are a great tool, the problem is that any data needs to be interpreted, and when it's interpreted by human beings it can obviously be misinterpreted. I've certainly done that and so have many in Major League Baseball and professional baseball.

Here's what I think is the next phase, the next area of growth and development in Major League Baseball, actually in all of baseball – implicit learning and brain training. What I mean by that is actually viewing ALL training as a type of stimulus for the neuromuscular system. Using the analytics, and using all the more traditional stuff we know, to create more robust learning environments. We believe we must actually view our training as a stimulus for the nervous system to respond to, adapt to, react to and just as importantly to customize and hyper-personalize that stimulus.

Case in point, Justin Verlander is one of my clients. If you follow baseball you would know that J. V.'s on the back half of his career. The way he trains, the way he moves, the way he needs to work is different than when he was 25 or 26. So not only are players different from each other, they're different from themselves over the course of their career. So even the same person is going to need to change and constantly adjust and customize his/her training.

Trying to create robust, hyper-personalized training that fits each and every individual is the way of the future. Sabermetrics will be a part of that but it won't be the lead part. It will be the information part. The far tougher and more valuable parts are in the assessment and then the execution/implementation of that hyper-personalization.

I've been lucky enough to get a lot of great advice in my career and hang around some pretty incredible people. I've tried to pass along as much as possible to the young pitching coaches, their pitchers and their parents.

Becoming Your Own Best Pitching Coach

I think the best advice I could give a pitcher is for him to become his own best pitching coach which requires him to do his due diligence. Find people on the way that can help you with some of the questions, but never, ever, ever, acquiesce completely to your trainer or your instructor because this is your career. You must determine who you are and what you believe.

Yes, you're going to need help, and advice, and guidance. You're going to need mentors. That is good. Go seek them out. But at the end of the day, you yourself are the ultimate decision maker and it needs to be your program, your thought process and your belief system. You need to become your own best pitching coach so you know who you are.

I see a lot of young guys go from one mentor to the next to the next. They're searching for the perfect mentor, and in my opinion, this is a path fraught with danger. They need to think of their mentor as their guide. The fact is, there are no absolutes and no one is going to know you, better than you.

Over the past twenty years, I've tried very diligently to incorporate this philosophy personally for myself. I actually pride myself in my ability to listen to almost anyone talk about pitching and listen intently without judgement because I already know who I am and I know what I believe. At the beginning of the conversation, I obviously don't know what they understand and what they believe, so I'm open to listen and this allows me to sort through and choose what I like, what I have little interest in and what I think is definitely less effective or flawed. It also allows me to think: "Hmm, I really need to think through this. Maybe I should put it on the back burner, and look at it a little more before I have an official position on this."

In my experience, when you do that, it gives you your best chance to grow and develop. When you're on the mound at Yankee Stadium in October, and you're facing the Red Sox, and it's bases loaded, it's all about you. It's not about anybody else and you're going to have to figure this thing out.

We've seen a lot of kids come through the Texas Baseball Ranch who are very talented and his parents maybe thinking, "You know I believe he might be special. He could actually become a Major Leaguer." I think it's so important to give those parents the type of advice I'd want if it were my son.

Choosing the Right Mentor is EVERYTHING

Here's what I tell them: For everything in life, whether it's medical advice, financial advice, or baseball advice, the first step I think all parents should take, is to do their due diligence. Choosing the right mentor is EVERYTHING. Don't just hire the guy that's closest to you, or the guy that had a good playing career, or a guy that was a star in your area. Do your due diligence. Really look through it and sort through it.

The second thing is to always use common sense in your decision making progress. If it sounds too good to be true, it almost always is. Be careful of wild promises, and be especially careful of "one size fits all" solutions. If success is really a one size fits all thing, then why wouldn't we all be successful? We'd just have to find the recipe and we're good to go. If only it were that simple. You need to really do your due diligence, use common sense, and stay away from one size fits all philosophies.

I love baseball. Baseball really has been my life. When I look at what we've done over the years, the players we've worked with, the impact we've had and the lives we've touched, baseball is what has been the teacher. Baseball is full of life lessons. I believe you can dream as big as your talent and work ethic will take you. We're not just training pitchers. We're sharing life lessons.

The Chien-Ming Wang Story

Earlier I mentioned Chien-Ming Wang. His story is one that I'll take with me the rest of my life. Here's a guy who was a Cy Young runner-up, suffers a devastating injury, and is out of organized baseball entirely. His agent reached out to me, I did my due diligence and we knew we could help him. It's funny, we could barely communicate but we really hit it off. And between Randy Sullivan and me, we did help him. We helped his arm health, and he ended up throwing harder at the age of 36 than when he was a 19-game winner with the Yankees, and he made made it all the way back to the Majors Leagues.

And because he was so important to baseball in Taiwan, a filmmaker followed his recovery efforts, and made a documentary about it. So not only were we able to help him get back, we were able to see all the people who were affected by his comeback. I even got to go to the premier of the movie in LA. That day, being Chien-Ming's coach made me a star to an audience full of Taiwanese people who idolized the man. I could have run for mayor that day and I would have won by a landslide. What a special experience that was.

This One Is For You Pop!

What a special life I've been able to live. My dad got me into baseball. He has passed away, but a week doesn't go by when I don't think about playing catch with him. That scene at the end of "Field of Dreams" really hits home with me and always makes me misty eyed. I know he'd been very proud of me and what we've been able to accomplish in the game.

I did this book for dads like mine, and all parents who want to see their sons do the best they can in baseball. This is a special game. I'm lucky to work with, and be friends with, some truly special people.

The people interviewed in this book share my passion for the game, and desire to help young pitchers see their dreams come true.

I tried to ask them the questions you would ask if you had the opportunity. So enough about me, let's hear from them.

ON THE

BUMP

CHAPTER 2

BRENT STROM

Brent Strom is the pitching coach of the Houston Astros. He played a major role in the team's 2017 World Series title, and their return to the World Series in 2019. In 2018, Brent led the Astros pitching staff as they set a Major League record with 1,687 strikeouts. The 2018 Astros also led Major League Baseball in virtually every significant category, including team ERA,
starter's ERA, bullpen ERA, and opponent average. For his efforts, Brent was named Baseball America's 2018 MLB Coach of the Year.

This is Brent's third stint as a Major League pitching coach, and second with the Astros. He also held that title with the Kansas City Royals. He previously was moved up to pitching coach for the Astros after seven seasons as a minor league pitching instructor. Brent also served as the minor league pitching coordinator and a minor league pitching instructor for the St. Louis Cardinals, was a pitching coordinator with the San Diego and Montreal/Washington organizations, and a minor league coach with the Los Angeles Dodgers.

Brent entered coaching after a 12-year pitching career, including five Major League seasons with the New York Mets,

Cleveland, and San Diego. During his playing career, Brent became just the second person to have Tommy John surgery. He attended the University of Southern California, leading them to two NCAA championships.

From 2018-2019, Brent was the oldest pitching coach in Major League Baseball, but developed a reputation for marrying an old-school baseball mentality with an open-minded approach to new-age analytics.

Ron: Brent, you've had a lot of success in your career, especially with the Astros, where you won the World Series and in 2018 you were named Major League Baseball Coach of the Year. Congratulations on that, it's well deserved.

When you started out, did you ever think you would end up at this high level, and experience what you've experienced?

Brent: First of all, thank you for your kind words on the Coach of the Year award. Just to put this in perspective, a lot of the same things I'm teaching now got me fired previously.

Early in my career, it was a case of perceived radical ideas such as using a vertical approach in attacking hitters, eschewing the sinker for the "straight" 4 seam fastball among other things. There were misunderstandings of some of the concepts I had learned from people outside the game and applied in professional baseball. So, while it's nice to be recognized now, I always refer back to what Bill Parcells once said, "Writers write, coaches coach, and players play." I've been blessed to have some of the best in the game to work with these past few years who bought into some of what I brought to the table, but rest assured it is the talent that makes theories work. So I think the credit really goes to them.

Ron: You've had many years of coaching and teaching, and you've overcome many challenges, that all helped you become who you are today. Talk about some of those experiences, and how it brought you to where you are now.

Brent: I would be the first one to admit that a lot of the teaching I did early in my career wasn't close to what it is today. I believe that's true of all coaches. Early on, we're not as informed as we could be, and we haven't looked outside our own little clique to see whether there are different ways of looking at things.

For instance, you can look to track and field, with javelin throwers or shot-putters and see where, for example, timing of the lead leg brace in the javelin or the rotational capabilities of the elite shot putter might indicate how velocity might be increased in throwing a baseball. If you look at the movement in a lot of different sports, it can be applied to baseball. I think the biggest thing that's helped me, not to mention you and others in our quest to help young pitchers get better, is to not just rely on what we think we know. I live my daily life realizing "I don't know what I don't know". I always questioned the idea that just because someone played the game, played it at a high level with success would necessarily have better ideas to share than someone who didn't play. It is the content, the presentation and the attention to detail that today's athlete is looking for. That said, I listen to everyone, sift through the information and see if it fits into my philosophy as it stands today. However, I reserve the right to change and that is where the Ranch has been a major contributor to what I presently believe. I want to have a large toolbox from which to pick for each individual under my trust. Not a one size fits all.

Ron: You're known for always looking at new ways to think and new ways to do things. You're always being innovative. And yet, as we talk today, you're the oldest pitching coach in the majors.

Brent: Yes, I am. Not sure that is a badge of honor or I was late to the dance...ha. It's been quite a journey. I started my coaching career when I was 30, thinking that I would be in the prime years of a stellar ML pitching career. Didn't pan out as I had thought but I loved the game and started my journey into coaching with the Dodger organization.

I went from pitching against to coaching the Albuquerque Dukes in the Pacific Coast League. That was a great stroke of luck for me because they were a pitching-oriented organization. I was able to learn from the likes of Sandy Koufax, and the late Don Drysdale, Johnny Podres, and other truly great pitching minds who helped get me started on the right track. That was really the start of my quest to educate myself, particularly in the field of biomechanics, arm health and velocity enhancement.

Ron: Along the way, is there one lesson you learned that stands out?

Brent: You can't have a generic program. Each individual is unique, in the way they move, the way they deliver the baseball, and countless other ways. As a coach, you have to unlock those things. And a lot of times the eyes will deceive you in terms of what you see. This has never been more apparent than working with my present team, the analytically oriented Houston Astros.

Case in point, Max Scherzer. When he was with the Diamondbacks, they thought for sure that he would hurt himself, so they traded him to Detroit. I see him as having one of the really good deliveries in baseball, even though to the eye it looks a little bit different. I think you need to slow things down. You need to utilize the technology that's available to slow things down so you can actually see what's really happening, and not just draw conclusions based on what your past tells you on what a delivery should look like and how people should drill.

Ron: I apologize for coming back to your age, but as we talk today you're 70 years old. You're a pitching coach in the majors, working with guys in their 20s. You're seeing the kids in their teens trying to get to the big leagues. And you're relating to them. You're working with them, you're guiding them, you're helping them. Do you think your experience level is actually an advantage for you in situations like that?

Brent: Ron, I believe one of the most important things I remember about my short pitching career is how incredibly difficult it can be. I have never lost sight of that. We (pitchers) are the most important people on the field. As I tell my pitcher's, Vegas doesn't make odds on who is playing right field. When I talk to them, I don't dominate the conversation. I ask questions dealing with how they feel and what they feel. My basic job as a coach is to allow them to become their own best pitching coach. My purpose quite simply is, when they run into a speed bump, to help them navigate past it, and shorten their learning curve, helping get them back on track ASAP.

I laugh some concerning my ability to relate to these young people. Having never had children I view them as mine. I want them to have success, to relish their time with teammates and feel a sense of accomplishment for all the hard work done. Nothing is guaranteed in this game. It is a difficult game one built on failure. I pride myself on not succumbing to negativity.

I just want to do what I can to not impede their progress. I try to stay as positive as possible. Give them options, give them ways to navigate this minefield that's extremely laden with things that could derail them. That's both on and off the field. It could be other coaches, it could be how they feel about themselves, it could be their mental and physical skills. It's all encompassing.

One reason I'm able to relate is that I realize how difficult it is to be a major league pitcher. Obviously, I didn't have the greatest of careers. I did the best I could. The injuries forced an early retirement for me. So I'm very aware of the dreams of these young people, and how hard they're working to get there.

My only gripe I have with the young players on the team is the pre-game music I hear from my office. I long for a little Frank Sinatra.

Ron: I'll second that.

You mentioned injuries in your case. You were actually the second person to have Tommy John surgery. You had it a few years after Tommy did.

One of the big things in pitching and in sports in general is keeping them healthy and making sure they can play. A lot of what you do as a pitching coach has changed over the years in terms of how you work with them. It's a lot more science and efficiency-based in how to use the body. Talk a little about that.

Brent: Funny thing about being the second guy, not many people know that about me. On the other hand, I saw Buzz Aldrin on TV the other night. I always ask people if they know what he's known for, and very few people know that he was the second man to walk on the moon. So I'm in good company.

While I certainly wasn't happy about needing the surgery, because it cost me dearly in my playing career, it did lead me on a path of trying to understand how the body moves, how the arm action can be improved, and how we can try to stop the onslaught of this injury.

I think one of the next frontiers will be in trying to meld the actual movement patterns that we try with what goes on in the weight room. Using how we strength train to try to change movement patterns. Strength itself isn't the key. You mentioned efficiency. There are certain people who are very efficient in the way they deliver the baseball. Sometimes I'm frustrated when I try to teach a movement pattern, and the player is trying and cannot do it. It's not a question of me not presenting the information correctly, or the pitcher himself not wanting to do it. It is the fact that he can't do it because of whatever limitations he may have. It may be his mobility, it may be stability of the back leg, it could be any number of things that we need to identify and then work on.

Now the weight room becomes part of the teaching process for these movement patterns. I think that's the next frontier we're trying get to. In fact, the Astros are trying to do that right now. It's not a question of how strong a player can get to withstand the stress he puts on himself, but basically try to move correctly. It's an ongoing process.

I'd like to be able to take Dr. Andrews out of the business of doing Tommy John surgeries. And I think we can do that.

Ron: That's great. It comes back to what you said earlier about it not being one size fits all. Everyone's program has to be tailored to the player, his strengths, his weaknesses, his goals. While there are certainly regimens everyone goes through, there are many that only that particular player does that particular way.

A lot of what you and I do stems from a snowy night in Seattle in 2003, which just may have been a watershed moment for the way pitchers in America would be trained.

Brent: That's an appropriate word. You asked me to speak at your Coaches Bootcamp in Seattle. My talk focused on what I was doing at the time, which I had gotten from Tom House. As you know, he started this whole inspection of how we're supposed to throw. He had a lot of different terms like equal and opposite, and front-side glove, and things like moving off the rubber, not staying back. Things like that always intrigued me.

Someone else was invited to talk, Paul Nyman. He can be a harsh critic, so fortunately for me, he was delayed by weather and he wasn't there to listen to my talk. But you and I were able to listen to his.

We sat together in the back of the room, and were basically blown away by what he presented. He presented athleticism, he presented momentum, and he made a very compelling case that we didn't really know that much. What we heard that night basically changed our entire world in terms of the way we started to look at how people pitch.

There's a saying which he included in his talk. "The best way to ruin a pitcher is to make him a pitcher." Even one of the all-time greats, Koufax, once told me, "All we are, are specialized throwers."

So throwing became our number priority. Not pitching. How the body moves in throwing, and the fact that we're on a mound. We're basically just like shortstops or second basemen. It's just that we have a few stretches that don't allow us to move like an infielder does, or an outfielder, or a catcher.

So that night changed everything for us.

Ron: You've now taken part in more than 250 camps at the Texas Baseball Ranch. Your influence is incredible. In this book, we're hearing from other Major League coaches, and youth coaches and virtually everyone has brought up your name when they've talked about the camps. Talk a little about what you've done there, the impact it's had on young pitchers, and how it's helped you in your coaching career.

Brent: First and foremost, it's a fun time for me, to get to see those guys again, as well as other coaches in baseball and your coaches. We learn from each other. I also utilize the time working with these young people that are very eager, because quite frankly, when you're in professional baseball, you run into a lot of guys that don't want to take a chance on certain things. They don't want to take a chance on losing where they are, even if where they are is not where they should be.

Young people are more like a sponge or a blank slate. I'll try different things with them to see how it works out. So while they're getting the chance to work with a Major League coach, they're actually helping me as much as I'm helping them.

I also try to make it fun for them. Sometimes I'll just reflect back on my career and tell them funny stories. Or because I've worked with so many people in professional baseball, I can tell stories about some of the guys they've read about, or seen on television, and how those pros went through the same things these kids are going through.

You and Jill have been very good to me. Here's something not a lot of people know. When I was let go by the Nationals on the last day of spring training, for a while I had a tough time getting another job because of my age. You included me in many camps, to help me stay in the game and continue to progress and learn. Thank you for that.

I also like to see how the camps have evolved. No one has all the answers, but you have a lot more now than when you started, and you're getting more all the time. It's all about helping these kids succeed.

Let's say I was teaching a curveball station. My joy was seeing a young kid who had never thrown a curveball, all of a sudden spin the ball correctly. I would give them a little name. I'd say, "You're now known as Yellow Hammer or Senor Snappy", or another term for a curveball. It was great to put a smile on their faces, and it was worth everything to me to see them passing the test.

Ron: Speaking of success, there are other coaches in the majors, like Derek Johnson and Wes Johnson, who are also in this book, and Craig Bjornson, Doug White and Eric Binder, who were all influenced by you. What do you think about seeing them having this type of success?

Brent: I think it's a two-way street. It's been a common quest for knowledge. All of them bring their own particular strengths to the table. We help each other. Many times we do that without even trying to. There's another name that should be on that list, Paul Davis with the Mariners. When I'm on the phone with any of these guys, I always pull out a notepad and take notes. I never know what they're going to say that will strike a chord.

They're all deserving of where they are, through their hard work. For example, Wes Johnson transforming himself from the hitting guy. Derek Johnson's success in college. Doug White working his way up through the minor leagues. I signed Eric Binder, and one day he asked me if he should continue. I said, "No, go into the front office." Someday, he's going to be a GM.

They all took different paths, and they're on different paths now. They're going to continue. Who knows what's next? I'll be watching their progress. It's gratifying to see their success.

Ron: In your opinion, how far has pitching development come in the last 10 to 20 years?

Brent: It's monumental. With technology adding all the things it has, we may have tilted to a point where we've lost the art form of teaching our pitching. I think a lot of the old guys, like Seaver and others, understood how to do things intuitively. I think what's happening now is that technology has allowed us to speed up the process. There's Edgertronic, TrackMan, Rapsodo, Flightscope and all the different things that are available now. I know the Astros utilize every possible way of looking at how the ball comes out of the hand and what it does. We can identify things quicker.

For example, after the World Series in 2017, I talked to Koufax. He talks a lot about third time around. When he pitched, whether it was against an average player or someone like Mays or Clemente, he wasn't the same pitcher the third time he faced them. He had to be a different pitcher.

Today, with all the numbers and data, we have a tendency to utilize the objective feedback and make it so strong that a decision is just going to be made. You may have six shutout innings, or even a no-hitter, but if the numbers indicate you're going to get your butt kicked shortly, they're going to take you out. I think sometimes we need to monitor that a little bit, and cruise back into what our eyes tell us and what we know about the pitcher himself.

If you have a stud guy, give him a little leeway even if the objective numbers tell you he's likely to get hit here. You have to use your eyes a little more. This has been a little difficult for me to accept, because I bridged that gap. I saw Nolan Ryan pitch. He had more than 200 complete games. I asked him, "Who was the best closer you've played with?" His answer: himself.

Even with all the technology, and what it's telling us, I think it's going to bend back slightly. I hope so. Hopefully, we won't lose that idea of allowing these pitchers to throw more complete games, or stay in there longer, depending on the efficiency factor.

Ron: There's that word efficiency again. It's just so critical. What do you see as the big thing that's going to evolve and improve over the next few years in professional baseball?

Brent: I touched on it earlier. I think the strength and conditioning, making sure what we do in the weight room lines up more with the delivery. I think that's going to be huge. And we'll see what other things will come into play. For example, I've been advocating Pilates, ballet, yoga, things like that. I think that's a frontier that needs to be explored with these pitchers even though they may not embrace it a great deal.

I think continuing to build the athleticism of the pitchers is going to be the number one thing. If somebody asked me whether I want a pitcher with exquisite timing, or one with great strength, I'll take the timing. I'll take the timing of the movement pattern. I think that's where we need to look.

We're already seeing that with a lot of different devices that are out there, 3D devices, the Motus sleeve, etc. There's all this digitizing taking place on guys right now. There's biokinetics. The big thing is to see it, but then what can we do with it? Where will the coaches' energy have to be directed? How can they change a movement pattern to enhance a pitcher's efficiency? Of course, it's like me trying to walk differently now, after I've been walking the way I have for 70 years. It's pretty difficult the older you get. But I think at the younger levels, this can be done quite easily, so that's where we need to start. I truly believe this is going to be the next frontier.

Ron: What's the best advice you ever got as a coach or a player?

Brent: To know when to shut up. To know when to not say anything. I think some of the best coaches know when to shut the hell up and let the players feel things. To not critique every little movement that may go wrong. Realizing they're human beings, and they'll never throw a baseball exactly the same ever again in their entire life. The body is too complex.

And to allow failure to take place. Learn from failure and don't be afraid of it.

Ron: What advice would you give a young aspiring pitcher? The kid, we'll call him, who may be in high school, may be in college, or may be starting out in the minors. His goal is to get to the majors, or at least have a good solid career. What advice would you give him?

Brent: You referenced college. I compare it to the fact that when we go to college, we have a major. Of course, scouts are looking for velocity and arm strength. That's going to be your major. Velocity is really the key to the kingdom, and the way you're going to get noticed. Scouts just aren't going to sign someone who's topping out at 82 miles an hour. The reason is, 82 miles an hour will also affect the off-speed pitches and other things that you learn.

So my suggestion for the young pitchers is, while your major may be improving your efficiency to be able to throw harder and get noticed, take out a very strong minor or a double major. Start to learn the changeup at a young age. Learn to throw the proper breaking ball with the proper spin. Because at the major league level right now, from what I'm noticing and what the objective feedback will tell me, is less fastballs are being thrown than ever before.

As such, the fastball is utilized as a weapon to get ahead in the count. It's a weapon to get foul balls. It's a weapon to get to two strikes. But it's not the weapon that puts people away. So understand off-speed, understand where hitters lines are, things like that. Take out that double major. Understand that while you're trying to improve your velocity or trying to improve your arm strength, do not fail to give equal energy to the other aspects. Focus on learning them, to improve your toolbox and have the weapons that can get major league hitters out, which includes all the off-speed pitches that are required to pitch at the highest level.

Ron: Good advice. Last question: what's your favorite baseball movie?

Brent: I would say *Field of Dreams*. Even though I was once talking to Kevin Costner, and asked him which of his baseball movies he liked most. He said, *"Field of Dreams* was my best movie, but I really liked holding Susan Sarandon in *Bull Durham*." That would certainly sway someone's opinion. But for me, it's *Field of Dreams.*

CHAPTER 3

JERRY WEINSTEIN

Jerry Weinstein has one of the most broad and diverse baseball resumes you'll see. It spans 50-plus years as a coach, manager, scout and other positions in professional baseball, college, and international competition. In  recognition of his accomplishments, Jerry received Baseball America's *Tony Gwynn Lifetime Achievement Award* in 2018.

Jerry does scouting and player development for the Colorado Rockies. He previously was in charge of minor league player development for the organization, and, at the age of 73, managed the Rockies' Double-A team in the Eastern League.

Jerry also served as Director of Player Development for the Los Angeles Dodgers.

His minor-league managing career includes stints in the Gulf Coast League, New York-Penn League, Cape Cod League, and California League. Jerry's college coaching career includes UCLA, the University of Miami, and Sacramento City College, which he led to 831 wins across 23 seasons, 16 league titles, one state title and one national title.

Jerry coached on the U.S. team that won the bronze medal in the 1996 Summer Olympics, and coached Team USA to a gold medal in the 2005 Maccabiah Games.

He is a member of the American Baseball Coaches Association Hall of Fame. Jerry co-authored *Baseball Coach's Survival Guide: Practical Techniques and Materials for Building an Effective Program and a Winning Team* with Tom Alston.

Ron: Jerry, you have a very deep and wide baseball career. You've been coaching or managing in professional baseball since 1989, and spent more than 20 years coaching at colleges before that. You've seen multiple trends come and go. Talk about the depth of experience you bring to your current role with the Rockies.

Jerry: I've been coaching in one form or another for more than 50 years. Even when I was a player, I'd always coach a team during the summer. Even if that was working for a recreation department. Early on, I knew my limitations as a player but I also knew I had a passion for the game, and my niche would be in coaching and teaching.

Ron: A lot of that has been working specifically with pitchers.

Jerry: If you're a manager or head coach, the scoreboard is important. Whether you're going to win or lose is largely going to be based on pitching. When I played, I was a catcher, so my job was to support the pitchers. The more information I had, the more trust they would have in me. For me, the man with the most information wins. So I've always had to do everything I could to get information. I've always had a growth mindset, and been an information junkie.

Ron: You received quite an honor when you were named the 2018 winner of the Tony Gwynn Award. That says a lot about what you have done over the years in baseball.

Jerry: That was totally unexpected. When the Baseball America people called to tell me I received the award, I said, "Really? Me?" I was almost embarrassed. Cal Ripken was the first recipient. So I'm receiving an award that Cal Ripken got, named after Tony Gwynn, who was at the top of the list as far as being an exemplary player, and more important, an exemplary person. I'm just honored and humbled to have received that.

Ron: It was very well-deserved. You talked earlier about being an information junkie. I always describe you as a voracious learner and a lifelong student. Those characteristics helped you keep going in your career, and make it to a level not many people reach. Let's talk about young coaches, and how important those characteristics are to them, as they desire to move up the ladder in competitive baseball.

Jerry: Let's face it, the more you know, the less you really do know and the more you need to know. Unfortunately, when we're young, we think we have all the answers. There's a saying in baseball that you're either humbled or you're about to be humbled, because that's a reality in this game. For me, the more I coached, the more I understood how much I didn't know and how much I needed to know.

If I'm going to be effective in bringing about change within players, which is really my job, one of the biggest things you have to understand is that one size doesn't fit all. You have to deal with the individual differences of the players. Of course that's not just in baseball, it's in any business. So you better have information, because without it, they won't trust you to affect a change in their performance. They may like you, but they won't trust you with their development. You need to have their trust.

I've also understood that it's more about the players than it is about you. It's a collaborative effort. And ultimately, as a coach or teacher, your job is to eliminate your job, not to create codependent players. Because there are so many varied personalities and skill sets out there, you have to have a wide ranging toolkit to accommodate each person. So it's critical to gather information so you can meet the needs of the individual player or student.

Ron: As you said, it's not one size fits all. That's a common theme I've heard from everyone in this book. You can't just take a player and fit him into a program, you have to tailor the program to fit the player. Is that different today than it was when you started out?

Jerry: I think the application is different today. We've always said, "He has good mechanics." Well, I don't even know what good mechanics are anymore. It's important to note that as a college or professional coach, by the time you'd get these players, they're already 15-year veterans of their sport. To think we can mold them into a particular form that is universal for everybody just is not possible because they've accommodated and adjusted along the way to meet the needs of their nervous system, or their biology, their physiology, and so on.

Ron: You recently spent a number of years managing at the AA level. That's such an important position in baseball, because it's a critical stage for a young player's development.

Jerry: That's the jumping off point for a big league player. Once you get to AA, you have a realistic expectation that you're going to play in the big leagues. But I try and create value within every player. This is not an exact science. And when we start to think, "This guy's a prospect and this guy isn't," my job is to help every player be as good as they can be. And, certainly at that AA level, they're at a crossroads, they're very close to being big league players. There's probably more movement today from Double A to the big leagues than ever before.

Ron: Why is that?

Jerry: I think the way things are structured right now, with the "win now" mentality and the raw tool sets in AA baseball, the transition to the big leagues is not as great as it used to be. The arms in AA may not be as refined as in AAA, but they're every bit as good. The only difference between AA and the big leagues is you're seeing those guys on a more consistent basis and they're more polished.

Ron: We go through cycles in baseball. Where do you think we are right now? Are we in a pitching dominant cycle? If that's the case, are we coveting velocity, command, better secondary stuff or is it all of the above.

Jerry: It's always a little bit of everything, and it depends. I think the one constant is people are hunting velocity, and we see it with a great jump in velocity. We're also seeing it in the changes in the way bullpens are structured today. Not too long ago it was, "Hey, take the starter out to sea and get into that bullpen. Now we're getting in the bullpen and each guy throws harder and, has more power. From a pitching standpoint, it's both power and finesse. There's actually kind of a contradiction, because we're seeing a great increase in velocity, but we're also seeing a great decrease in fastball usage. We're at the lowest fastball usage we've ever been at.

That speaks to the point of contrast and pitchability, and in secondary pitches, and how tough it is to adjust from high velocity to contrast with a lower velocity, and being on time as a hitter. So the value of mixing speeds is becoming more important, even though the mixture is from high 90's to low 80's, instead of, maybe five years ago, when it was 90 miles an hour to 80 miles an hour. There's still that contrast. But, when the ball is coming at 98 or 99 miles an hour, the milliseconds you have to make a decision and pull the trigger are not very long. That the amount of distance you see, and information you get, are not very great. So now, the contrast between fast and slow is even greater.

Ron: Obviously one of the most important things for a pitcher is being healthy enough to actually pitch. In the conversations throughout this book, we've talked a lot about mechanical efficiency, about moving better. If you can throw 100 miles an hour, but you can't stay healthy what good is it? You need to have the velocity, but you have to stay healthy and you have to be able take the ball when it's offered to you. Do you think there's been more emphasis on that in the last 10 years?

Jerry: I'm not sure we've even scratched the surface on keeping pitchers healthy. If you look at the disabled list every year, 42 percent of the people on it are pitchers. I think that's a black hole right now in professional baseball. We really don't fully understand what it takes to keep pitchers healthy. Or if we do, we haven't found the key to the treasure chest as yet. I think that's an ongoing battle. But, I do feel with the new technologies we have, with the diagnostic tools and the analytics we have, and it being a priority, especially with the high cost of pitching, that we're headed in the right direction as far as unlocking some of the secrets in that area.

Ron: I'm glad you brought up the high cost of personnel in professional baseball. Some of us remember when baseball had its first million dollar pitcher. Now you have 100-million dollar pitchers. That's an expensive piece of the puzzle for a baseball team, and not being able to use one of their best arms is a problem for any organization.

Jerry: That's what's driving the agendas now. We have to not only produce power and strength, but we also have to find to find a way to keep that power and strength on the field. We have to find better ways relative to rest, rehab, all the other things that are going on in terms of keeping people healthy.

Ron: Over the last 25 years or so, you've spent a lot of time with many of the thought leaders in baseball. Guys like

Tom House, Mike Marshall, Paul Nyman, Bill Thurston, Brent Strom and Derek Johnson who are both in this book with you. Talk about the guys that have been the most influential to you in your development, in your career.

Jerry: All of the above to a certain degree. But I think Paul Nyman has had a big effect on everybody on that list. I think Paul, in terms of intent, points out that with pitchers, first you need to learn how to throw before you learn how to pitch. It's pitching with aggressiveness and intent. And, I think part of that intent, as a byproduct, is that pitchers are pitching with much different tempo today. It used to be slow down and stay back and get to a balanced position. Now, it's about momentum. Our leading coach is Isaac Newton. It's relative to the laws of motion. So now, people are being more athletic. Their deliveries are more athletic.

Which I think is kind of a throwback to the way guys used to pitch. Bob Gibson and Whitey Ford and guys like that, used to pitch much more up-tempo. Less control, less balanced, and now we're getting back to that. And then, we're kind of backwards engineering the delivery based on the outcome. What does a pitch look like in terms of velocity, location, movement? What kind of reaction are you getting from the catchers? What kind of reaction are you getting from the hitters? Then backwards chaining and looking at that pitcher and what his movement pattern looked like on that particular pitch. Those are his particular mechanics. But I think we're encouraging pitchers to be a lot more athletic and a lot less robotic, and a lot less pitch by the numbers. I think Paul was one of the first guys who talked about intent, so he had a great effect on it. Then all the other guys have added their own piece relative to that as well.

Ron: You share your knowledge a lot. You've presented many times at coaching clinics, including the largest one in the world, the ABCA. Obviously the people who listen to you get a lot out of it. What do you get out of doing this?

Jerry: I get the satisfaction of knowing I'm helping other people. Because I wouldn't be where I am if it weren't for people like you, and Brent, and DJ, and Paul Nyman, and Kenny Myers, and Lloyd Christopher. Back in the day, when I grew up in LA, after a game, the scouts would sit around and talk all the time and young guys would just sit there and listen. They were reminiscing and talking, but we were learning. So I think it's payback time. I want to help other people just like they did. Maybe it wasn't by design, but they helped me be who I am today.

Ron: You've seen many developments over many years, but for this question, let's only go back five years or so. What are a couple of the biggest or most important changes in training which you've seen in these last couple years?

Jerry: I think we understand better what's happening biomechanically, especially in the shoulder and elbow joint. What are the things that can help us maximize our arm speed, and also minimize our injury risk? Not that we're going to totally minimize injury risk or maximize arm speed, but we understand the biomechanics a little better because of the new motion studies, the faster cameras, and the smarter, more educated, less anecdotal people that are getting involved in our game. It's not, "Well, I pitched this way, and I did this," which they really didn't understand. I think we're gaining a greater understanding of the total process, not only from the physical standpoint, but from the psychological standpoint.

Years ago there wasn't nearly the sports psych presence there is in the game today. And, I think that's a critical element, because in reality, there are four areas that people develop, the technical, the tactical, the physiological and the psychological. The technical is more of a mechanical thing. The tactical is more of a strategical approach to pitching. The physiological is more strength and conditioning. And then, the psychological is the mindset, and that pretty much controls everything.

Ron: That's really interesting. No one I've talked to so far has said that. That's something everyone should pay attention to.

So now that I've asked you to look back, let's shift the focus and look forward. Are there a couple key things which you think are going to evolve and improve the most in professional baseball over the next few years?

Jerry: I think we have a disconnect, not just in baseball, but most things that occur in the world today. It's called cause and effect. We're not able to take John Q. Left-handed Pitcher and say, "Hey, if you do this, this is going to happen." There are so many variables out there. But I think we're going to get better at delineating cause and effect. We're going to eliminate a lot of those variables, and we're going to be able to customize drills and movement patterns for individual players that are going to get direct results. There will be less and less guesswork because we have better technology in terms of diagnostics.

Pitch design is such a big part of today's pitcher development plan. With all the spin data, such as spin rate, spin axis and true spin, that we generate from Rapsodo and Trackman in conjunction with the Edgertronic high speed video, we've been able to fill in a lot of the spaces between the dots relative to each individual pitcher. Combine that with all the statistical data, and we are better able to customize a plan of attack that best meets the needs of each pitcher. Once each pitcher maximizes his skill set through all these technological & data advances, the disconnect is still the ability of the pitcher to execute the pitch. We are still not there, in that Major League pitchers only hit their target, which is less than a 3.8inch miss, with fastballs only 24 percent of the time.

Also, from a coaching aid standpoint, and this is very futuristic, I think there's going to be some type of an ecto-skeleton support that will reduce injuries. Whether that's some type of taping apparatus, or whatever. And I don't know if this will be good or bad, because we might end up with guys throwing 120 miles an hour, but in some way, I think we're going to better support that ligament from an external standpoint. There's a lot of work going on at MIT in their biomechanical lab. We'll see. Again, this is pretty futuristic stuff.

But, I believe baseball, and for that matter athletics in general, has never been better. We've got more smart people involved. We're getting more and more diverse. There's less inbreeding, especially in baseball. Fresh ideas are good, and If you look at all the recent hires, we're getting more outside people coming into the game. Guys who have not played professional baseball, or at least have not played in the big leagues. I think that's a good thing because we're getting new ideas. And I think the combination of the old guard that's been there and done that, combined with the new thinking and new analytics, is going to really help us grow our game faster than it's ever grown.

Ron: I look forward to that. What's the best advice you've ever gotten in your baseball career?

Jerry: To listen. You need to shut up and listen. That, and be open minded. The smart man learns more from the dumb man than the dumb man learns from the smart man. You can learn from everybody. Listen to your players. Watch your players. We learn more from our players than we do from anybody else. It's a sounding board for what you are doing. And you have to understand it's a partnership. It's a collaborative effort. It's so important to pay attention to what's going on with your players.

Ron: If you were being asked for advice by a young coach, perhaps one in college or at the lower levels of the minors, who wants to advance his career, is that the advice you would give him?

Jerry: I think the number one thing is to get as much information as you can get. Learn as much as you can, read as much as you can, study as much as you can, spend as much time as you can on the Internet. I think that's a great teaching tool. There's some unbelievable information out there. But you have to filter it. Not only do you have to filter it for yourself, you have to filter it for your players, because they're doing the same thing you're doing. They're out there getting information, and they have 10 million things swimming around in their cranium. You have to identify those things that are best for them, because they'll try anything. You have to isolate things and keep it simple.

But you just can't have too much information. That doesn't mean you're going to use it, but at least you have it in your file cabinet. Maybe you're not going to use it today, or next month, or next year, but five years from now you may reach in there and say, "Hey, I remember this and I'm going to try this with this guy."

Ron: What advice would you give a young pitcher? He could still be in high school, college or starting his minor league career. He wants to make that step to the next level. How would you advise that young pitcher about his developmental path?

Jerry: I'd tell him he's responsible for his own development. Transfer of blame is not acceptable. You have to figure out what you need to do for you. You have to be willing to experiment. You have to be willing to fail, in order to succeed. There are going to be obstacles. The improvements are going to come in small increments. But ultimately, it's 100 percent your responsibility. It's who you surround yourself with, the type of information you sign off on and adopt for yourself. And the development process is never ending. It's slow and it's tedious and it takes time. How much time? Who knows? Not all the fruit on the tree gets ripe at the same time. Everybody's different. But if you work every day to get a little bit better, the improvements will come. A lot of young guys want it yesterday. They want the magic potion. They're not willing to plateau or get worse in order to get better.

Ron: Very well said.   Last question. What's your favorite
         baseball movie?

Jerry: It's funny, I love sports movies, and I don't have a
         baseball movie in my top five. I loved *Remember the
         Titans*, and *Hoosiers*, and *Glory Days*, inspirational
         movies about underdogs. But for baseball movies, I
         liked *Bull Durham* an awful lot. Most baseball movies
         just lack realism for me. They haven't struck that
         chord. But I did like *Bull Durham.*

CHAPTER 4

DEWEY ROBINSON

Dewey Robinson is minor-league pitching coordinator for the Tampa Bay Rays. He was promoted to that position after serving as a minor league pitching instructor for the organization for eight years. Dewey previously was a Major League pitching coach for the Houston Astros and bullpen coach for the Chicago White Sox. He also served as Chicago's minor league pitching coordinator, and pitching coach at two of the team's minor league affiliates.

Dewey Robinson

During his stint with Tampa Bay, Dewey has become known for developing pitchers. In 2019, Tampa Bay compiled a staff ERA under 4.00 for the ninth time in 10 seasons, and 2011 draft pick Blake Snell won the Cy Young Award in 2018.

Dewey coached collegiately at Northwestern University and the University of Missouri. He entered coaching after a playing career that included pitching in 30 Major League games in relief for the White Sox over three seasons.

Ron: Dewey, you've been a pitcher and a coach at the college level, and both the minor and major leagues, so you have a broad range of experience in baseball. During your 35-plus years of coaching, you've seen a lot of trends come and go. Talk about that, and how your depth of experience helps you in what you're doing now.

Dewey: Not long ago, I did a presentation at the Texas Baseball Ranch, and as you know, I ended with computers and cameras. I feel those two things, and how they've evolved, have changed baseball, and all sports, dramatically.

When I first started coaching, I would sit with a calculator and paper and pencil at the end of the year to total up numbers and statistics. First pitch strikes, one-and-one counts, ahead, behind, strike percentage, all of it by hand. And the video cameras we used back then were only 30 to 40 shots per second.

Now, with the push of a button on a computer, all these stats are instant. You could have 10 years of data instantly. And the cameras we are using now are 950 shots per second, so we're seeing everything, and we're able to record everything.

It's amazing how it's changed over the years. The more we see, the more data we get, and the more we can study things, the more our coaching philosophies change, because now we can see things we never could before. We can see how the ball comes off fingertips and what kind of spin there was. 20 years ago, we were always guessing because the cameras weren't good enough.

Look at the athletes today. They're better than they were 30 years ago. They're stronger and they're quicker, and I think it's because we're more educated on how we can train them to be better. Whether it's nutrition, sleep, strength, efficiency, mechanics, all that goes hand-in-hand.

Look back to when I was coordinating with the White Sox in the early '90s. Out of 100 pitchers in our system, if I had five or six throwing 90 miles an hour, that was a lot. Now, out of 100 pitchers in our Rays system, there aren't five pitchers that don't throw 90. Just about everyone's doing that. The average is now 94 miles an hour when it was probably 84 back then.

Because we've learned so much through computers and cameras, we're able to coach better. I've always been a big fan of both. I've always studied statistics looking for an edge on how to teach pitching to a pitcher, how to teach counts, and what's efficiency. I've always looked at video trying to see what the good pitchers do. Are there similarities that help them throw harder, throw more strikes, or have better breaking balls?

So to me, it keeps coming back to computers and cameras.

Ron: Let me follow up on that. As you now have much more information and get it so much faster, how are you able to use it? What are the changes in the actual training of the pitchers that have come along and really made a difference?

Dewey: I was pretty fortunate because when I started with the White Sox, we had a very innovative strength and conditioning guy, Vern Gambetta, who's gone on to do some wonderful things, not only in baseball but other sports. I was lucky to be around him. But the industry in general has taken that, and been able to specialize the training so the pitchers are getting specific workouts to get them stronger and quicker, so they can throw harder, throw more efficiently. On that end of it, that's been really good.

On my end of it, now being able to study mechanics and pitches and things like that so much better, I've seen some things that make me embarrassed about what I was teaching 20 or 30 years ago. I'll be the first to admit, you constantly have to look at yourself and you have to be constantly learning. There are always different ways of doing things.

Ron: You mentioned not just pitching harder but pitching more efficiently. That's something we've talked about a lot over the years.

Dewey: Let's start with spin efficiency. We might be able to get carry or vertical movement on a fastball and a four-seam fastball, but with the instruments we have access to now, like TrackMan and Rapsodo, we're looking for different ways to use the efficiency of the spin to get better vertical movement, something that we never would have had access to 10 years ago, let alone 20 or 30. That's the start of it.

            On the mechanical end, the fundamentals of the delivery, being able to really break down from high-speed video what is actually happening, and how it should happen, has changed my philosophy on how I teach mechanics too.

Ron: And that's so important, because as we dive into the science of this, we look into how they use their own bodies to not just throw harder and effectively, but also to be able to stay healthy and durable. We're doing everything we can to avoid those devastating injuries and keep pitchers healthier.

Dewey: That used to be the million-dollar question. With salaries today, it's the $100 million-dollar question or more. I always tell people, my number one goal with each pitcher that comes in our system is to keep him healthy. Number two is to get him to the big leagues.

If players get hurt and have surgery, that's missed time that they'll never get back. And you're never sure if they're going to come back as good as they were before they got hurt.

I'm close friends with Dr. Glenn Fleisig at Dr. Andrews' pitching lab. He and I always talk about these health issues. He constantly tells me that with the speed pitchers are throwing today, the ligaments and tendons can't really handle the forces being put on the ulnar nerve, and that's why there's always an increased risk of injury. These guys are too big and strong, and everything is moving so quickly. It's hard for the body to take this long-term.

So we try to do everything we possibly can to keep them healthy. We look at workload, mechanics, pitch efficiency, all those kinds of things. We're always trying to find the magic answer, but I don't know if it's there.

Ron: Earlier you talked about how many more pitchers are now throwing 90 miles an hour. Is the increase in speed the biggest change you've seen at the professional level? What other changes have you seen?

Dewey: Speed is definitely the biggest change I've seen. Also, with equipment like TrackMan, Rapsodo and all these cameras, we're looking at things like pitch efficiency, how to increase spin rate, and how to get the ball to move. That has really come into play in just the last five years or even less. It's become vogue in baseball to get the ball to carry, to really use your strengths, more so than it was in the past.

When I was pitching, and even just 10 or 15 years ago, it was more about getting guys to hit the ball on the ground with sinkers, things like that. That's still important. But what's transpired in the last four or five years is, from all the data that's being supplied now, you can pitch up in the strike zone and get a lot of swing and miss if you have vertical movement or good carry off your fastball.

20 years ago, we would call that deception. We didn't know why guys would swing and miss through a high fastball that looked pretty easy to hit, but it just wasn't. Now, with all the cameras and the data, they've figured that with the spin, the gravity pull isn't the same. It really is staying on line a little longer.

Ron: You're a frequent visitor to the Texas Baseball Ranch, and the Florida Baseball Ranch, and take part in many of the boot camps. Talk about the coaches' events and why you do this.

Dewey: It's all about learning. I have the utmost respect for you and Randy and all the guys. You can experiment and train guys a little more than I'm able to do, because once a guy's in our system, his career's on the line. It's more about keeping him healthy and getting him to the big leagues, while you're more in a training mode to try to get that guy to a certain level.

The relationship we've had over the years is really give and take both ways. We're each learning. I can keep up with what you're doing and why you're doing it, and pick up things I might use, and I'm always willing to share stuff that we do or we see, that you might use in the future too. It's all about learning, and trying to keep up to date with things.

Ron: That fits with the fact that I've always referred to you as a voracious learner and a lifetime student. How important do you believe those characteristics are to young coaches, whether they're at a high level of professional baseball or trying to get there?

Dewey: The first thing I always say to a young coach is read everything you can get your hands on, hang around coaches that you look up to, just try to learn as much as you possibly can.

I believe there are times I can learn more from a high school coach than one of my peers because he's dealing with different situations and different environments. He might be in a gym in Chicago, where he can't get outside, so he has to be innovative. He's thinking, "Okay, I have a gym for an hour and 20 pitchers, what can I do?" I'm constantly learning and looking for different ways to do things.

Ron: Is that the best advice you would give any young coach, keep learning and learn from everyone that you can?

Dewey: And don't forget reading. I'm constantly trying to find books on baseball or coaching or any type of teaching, because you never know when you're going to use this kind of stuff. You might be in the bullpen working with a kid and something might come to mind that you read in a book a year ago. "Hey, I dealt with this. This might work."

         One of the topics I brought up in my presentation was how my coaching philosophy is improvisation, and being able to think on your feet and not be afraid to fail. I'm always looking for new things to get my point across to a pitcher, something that might help him then, in the future or both.

Ron: You talk about learning from other coaches. You've presented at a lot of coaching clinics over the years, which means there are a lot of people learning from you.

Dewey: We're all sharing information. I'm always asking other pitching coaches, "What did you do when you had a guy that couldn't do this?" You're always looking for different ways to share or learn.

         When I present, first off I look at my audience and determine what audience it's for. "Is it high school, college, or pro? What are they looking for? What can I share with them that can help them and their pitchers going forward this season?" Because when I go to a conference, I want to be able to take something back that I can use in the future. So when I talk to these guys, my main point is, "Okay, I have some experience here. I have some things that have or haven't worked. How can I share them with these coaches so they can be better going forward?"

Ron: I asked you about the advice you give to young coaches. What about the pitchers? What advice would you give to young aspiring professional pitchers, the ones that are 16 to 22-years-old, as they move along this developmental path? Their goal is making it to the big leagues. Talk about what you say to them.

Dewey: That's the way I went through high school, college, and pro ball. I only had a short career in the big leagues, but I never wanted to sell myself short. I wanted to be able to finish whatever level I was at, and feel like I did everything I possibly could to go forward. If it ended after high school, after college, after the minor leagues, wherever it ended, I wanted to be able to live with myself and be happy with the work I put in, that I didn't leave anything on the table.

         That's what I try to tell young players. Stay in school and get your education. You never know how this is going to work out, but be content in how you approached your schooling and your baseball career and be able to live with yourself. If you've done everything you can when you're going through school or going through the minors, you can live with yourself afterwards and move on. You don't linger and keep trying to get back in the game thinking, "If only I worked a little harder, I would be a little better."

I've always said this about professional players, I wish we could release them for a day, just once, because it's amazing when you see a kid come back and get a second chance with you. What a difference in the approach or attitude. When you're a player, you think this is going to go on forever. But it could end tomorrow. You want to take that approach with it.

Ron: What's the best advice anyone ever gave you?

Dewey: It's not specific to baseball, but it fits. Be a good listener. I'm always trying to listen, and see what's going on inside a player's head. It's hard to lead kids today. You almost have to walk beside them as they're going through their journey or their struggles, so they have somebody there with them. 30 years ago, you could lead guys. Now you have to be with them.

It's all about being open and having an open mind. I do a lot of open-ended questions with kids and try to get them to open up so I can know, "Where is this kid coming from? What kind of environment? What kind of home life? What kind of work ethic does he have?" I try to approach it that way.

I would say that's what I get out of most of all the research, the reading, the talking to coaches. "Just shut up and listen." You learn more that way.

Ron: Earlier I asked you about the changes you've seen in baseball. Now instead of looking back, I'm going to ask you to get out your crystal ball and look ahead. Tell me, what do you think are the next big couple things that will evolve and improve over the next several years in professional baseball?

Dewey: It's actually scary to think about what could happen, because look at what's happened in the last five years. We were probably at a flat line for 30 years. Then with TrackMan and Rapsodo and KiniTrax and all these high-speed cameras, it's probably on a vertical movement straight up. The game has changed so much in the last five years, if you just look at shifts and the way guys are pitching and the arm strength and everything.

So what might happen in the next five or 10 years? On the hitting side, the way I look at it, they're really trying to adjust what the pitchers are doing to them because the strikeout rates are going through the roof and the game is changing there. I don't think I would have seen this coming.

Ron: The game always seems to go through cycles. Right now, we're in a cycle with record numbers of home runs and record numbers of strikeouts. If there was one thing that might be the big change a couple years from now, what do you think it might be?

Dewey: Let me put it this way. I'm hoping it gets back into more of the fundamentals of baseball. I've always thought the small things are vital to the game, and make it exciting. I'd like to see bunts, hitting and running, small ball, whatever you want to call it, stuff like that. I think it's much more interesting when the game is 4 to 3, 5 to 4, and there are a lot more balls put in play and there's a lot more action involved. There might be one home run and seven or eight strikeouts per nine innings instead of two home runs, 15 strikeouts per side.

This is a pitching guy talking, but as far as the entertainment side of things, I would say just reading into what the Commissioner's Office is talking about, they're concerned with the shifts and the amount of strikeouts because there is so much dead time. There's not a lot of balls put in play. They're trying to figure out ways to go about doing this. I don't know if they will, but I'm hoping those kinds of things become vogue again. Stolen bases, bunts, things like that, just movement on the baseball field to make it more interesting.

Ron: More interesting. That's a good answer. One last question. What's your favorite baseball movie?

Dewey: I'm going to go back to *Bull Durham*. I actually was fortunate enough in my first year of coaching professionally, to be in the Carolina League. Not in Durham, but we played there. And that winter was when they shot the movie. Being in the minors myself, I thought there was a lot in that movie that was pretty true to life. It was a story you could relate to.

Ron: I think a lot of baseball people could relate to it. Thank you Dewey Robinson, for sharing your story and your insights.

CHAPTER 5

DEREK JOHNSON

Derek Johnson is the pitching coach of the Cincinnati Reds. He was named to that position in November, 2018 as new manager David Bell assembled his staff.

Derek spent the previous three seasons in the same position with the Milwaukee Brewers. During that period, Milwaukee's cumulative ERA was the fourth-best in the National League and eighth-best in the Major Leagues. In 2018, Brewers pitchers set franchise records for strikeouts in a season and lowest opponent batting average.

Derek began his professional coaching career as minor league pitching coordinator for the Chicago Cubs. Previously he coached in the college ranks, including 10 years as pitching coach at Vanderbilt University, where he also served as associate head coach for three years. During that time Derek was named National Pitching Coach of the Year and National Assistant Coach of the Year, and helped lead Vanderbilt to its first College World Series appearance.

As a college coach, Derek mentored 13 pitchers who have appeared in the Major Leagues, and helped produce six first round/supplemental first round draft picks.

In 2012, Derek authored *The Complete Guide to Pitching.*

Ron: Derek, your background in baseball includes a piece of history not everyone is aware of; you were the first college coach with no professional baseball experience to be hired as a minor league pitching coordinator. That's pretty special and has since paved the way for several others.

You spent a lot of time coaching in college, so let's begin with that portion of your journey.

Derek: I was a college coach for 20 years and loved it. The last 10 were at Vanderbilt. It's a great school, a great baseball program, and I really didn't have any aspirations to go into the professional ranks. But then I had an opportunity with the Cubs and it was a point in my life where I felt I needed a new challenge. So I took the job and was their minor league pitching coordinator for three years. Then I had an opportunity to be a pitching coach in the majors with the Brewers. Now here I am with the Reds, so even though I didn't necessarily think I would ever be a professional coach, an opportunity came about and the rest is history.

Recently there's been more of an influx of college coaches who have gone into professional baseball as coordinators and pitching coaches. I think that's great. I think what's happened is they're seeing the value of what college coaches can do. I think they're seeing that college coaches are pretty highly trained in a lot of different areas, and they see the value in that. Before it was more closed off. If you played, you could coach.

Now I think they're looking at it as, the more highly skilled you are and the more highly trained you are, the more valuable you can be. They're looking at it from a value standpoint. "These coaches are really highly trained, and we need to figure out a way to get them involved in our organization."

Ron: Talk a little bit more about value in coaching. Can you also share some of the takeaways from college coaching that you brought with you to the pros and how those things may have opened up the professional ranks for others like you?

Derek: I think one thing that a college coach has that a professional coach, at least a few years ago probably didn't have, is the opportunity to try anything. We can study anything, and once we study it, we would try it, really with no backlash. If it worked, great. If it didn't, we failed and we'd try something else. There wasn't anyone looking over us saying, "You can do this. You can't do this."

So we were open to trying anything new. Then we'd either implement it with our college teams, or decide against it. That's probably something a pro coach couldn't do. He may have been interested in something, but really had to have permission in order to implement it into his system. There was just the hierarchy of it.

But now I think it's gotten to the point where they understand that there's a lot of information out there. There are a lot of things these college coaches have tried. They've implemented it into their teams and it's worked pretty well. So professional baseball is a little more apt to loosen the reins and let guys try these new things.

Ron: You certainly had no shortage of recognitions in your college career, including being named ABCA Assistant Coach of the Year at Vanderbilt. What did that mean to you?

Derek: It's an honor I'll forever cherish. I didn't necessarily want to be a head coach, so to receive that honor as an assistant coach was about the best you could do from an assistant coach standpoint. I certainly aspired to that honor, so it was truly great when I received it.

I wanted to be as good as I could possibly be from a pitching standpoint. And I was at a great place to do that. We had a great pitching staff. We did a great job recruiting. Tim Corbin is the head coach there and he was a great influence on me. He was a great mentor. I was able to take a lot from him in the way he approached things, and apply it to the pitching side.

I've learned from a lot of other people too, including you, Brent Strom, and other great minds I've met along the way. I was able to take things you all taught, and apply them to my situation.

Ron: I'm glad you talked about learning. I refer to you as a voracious learner and a lifelong student. Talk about the importance of that for any young coach who wants to move up the ladder and possibly get to where you are.

Derek: I love learning new things. I love opening new doors from a pitching standpoint. There's so much information out there. One thing I've learned about baseball over the years is there's just this ecosystem of information that's still uncovered. We haven't unearthed even a fraction of it. The reason is, you're dealing with people, and there are infinite things involved when it comes to people.

I love the idea of trying to figure out why. I think that's a big piece to being a coach. And there are "why's" for everything. Why a pitch does what it does. Why a person thinks the way they think. Why we have certain situations happen to us inside a game and out. I love the idea of understanding the "why" better. I think that's really what coaching is. I think it's taking your situation and trying as best we can to understand why things happen. I also love the idea of learning the new things. And there's so much new out there in baseball. We're uncovering more and more, but there's much more to be discovered. That's something I truly enjoy doing.

Ron: As we talk about things that are happening and things that are changing, let me ask you to do two things. Look back, and then look forward. First, talk about the shifts you've seen in the last 10 or 20 years in pitching development and pitching coaches. And then tell me the next couple big things you see coming down the pike in the next five years or so in professional baseball.

Derek: When I first started coaching, I did so based on my experience. I think that's true of any coach. You coach based on the type of player you were, so I used what I had learned up to that point and tried to apply it to my players. But I realized fairly quickly that most of the players I was dealing with were much different than I was. They thought differently than I thought. They certainly pitched differently than I pitched.

I felt like I was saying the same thing to every player that I was coaching. And you can't be one size fits all. So I began reading anything I could get my hands on, trying to become a better coach. I met you, and I began listening to Tom House. I thought his information was unbelievable. To this day, I still use some of it. It was not the traditional things that all the pitching coaches were talking about 25 years ago. It opened up a whole new world for me. The same for Paul Nyman. These were things I hadn't heard before.

New terms were being thrown out there. There were ways of pitching and ways of moving that I hadn't heard at that point.

I began learning all this new information and trying to figure out a way to apply it, and like any coach, you take what you learn, you put it into your situation and eventually you make it your own. That's something I think every coach has to ultimately do. For me, it was a way for me to, again, figure out the "why".

Along the way, more people began listening to this. There was a shift. It was a different paradigm. And that was very intriguing for me. Because frankly, with the other stuff, I walked away from a lot of different bullpens, or different games, or different seasons for that matter, thinking, "When it comes to pitching, is this all there is?" This opened up my world to new possibilities.

What you're seeing now is we're more advanced technologically. We have things at our disposal that we didn't have even just six or seven years ago. TrackMan has become a big piece to pitching, and it's explaining some things that we can't see with our naked eye, or even with a camera. This is movement with the ball, and you're talking about things that airplane pilots were talking about back in the day with Magnus force and that type of stuff.

In the next five or six years, I think you're going to see additional pieces to those technologies. I can tell you for the last two or three years, I've been interested in understanding ball flight. That's where TrackMan comes into play, and how we can use it to better serve our pitchers to help them understand what they do well, and maybe some things they don't do so well. We're developing different pitches because of that. We're developing designs on how to pitch against left-handed and right-handed hitters.

Biomechanically, there's more information about the way the body moves than ever before. Biomechanics have been around for a long time. But we haven't tried to apply it to the pitching motion the way we are now. We have a better understanding of the way the body moves. And if you take that even a step further to the coaching realm, now we're able to understand how to make our practices better to help our players move better in a much shorter amount of time. So instead of it being 30 or 40 trials, maybe we're cutting that down to 10. Now our production rate is going up. We're able to teach guys how to move better and we're doing that more quickly. And what's really key, at the same time we're able to help our players learn quicker.

Ron: Throughout the years, baseball has always had the high velocity guys like Sandy Koufax, Bob Feller, Bob Gibson, Nolan Ryan & Randy Johnson. But consistently, more pitchers today are throwing with velocities over 95 mph. 90 miles an hour used to be the minority, now it's the standard. With the use of science and technology to help them throw harder, we also have to help them move more efficiently. Ultimately the goal is to keep their arms healthier and make their careers longer.

Derek: A guy can't pitch better if he can't pitch at all because he's hurt. So there are a lot of layers to what we're trying to do. And you can even take it a step further. Yes, you have the science of pitching, but you also have the art of it. We have a lot of kids, whether they're 15 or 16, or 23 or 24, who are extremely strong, and who throw extremely hard, but haven't yet mastered the other side, which is the art of pitching. Throwing the ball where they want, and making it move the way that they want, and understanding how pitches work together, and things like that.

It's gamesmanship. It's the way that you approach a game to win. There's a thought process behind that as well. And I think we're losing some of that. We've kind of gone from one side to the other. For me, the best pitchers in the game, like the ones you mentioned, have figured out both sides. They're some of the best throwers in the game, but they're also some of the best pitchers in the game. They've learned the nuances of both the science and the art of it. In my mind as a coach, you have to kind of keep all those things in mind. And in the end, to be a professional pitcher, to be a Major League pitcher, especially to be a great Major League pitcher, it's more than just the technical aspect of throwing a baseball. There's a lot that goes into it.

Ron: What's the best advice you've ever gotten as a coach?

Derek: I think the best advice any coach could give to another is this: Relationships are your number one priority. That was given to me a long time ago, and it has stayed with me. If you can show that you're real, and show that you're in it for the long haul with a player, and you can be honest with him, whether you're being positive or negative, then you can become a good coach. We have all this great information, thanks to all the new technology we're using, but it can't help a player if you can't reach him. You can't reach him if he doesn't trust you. He doesn't trust you if there isn't that bond, that relationship.

I try to stick to those three principles when I'm dealing with a player. I want to be as authentic as I can. I don't want to come across as someone who is above him. I want to come across as someone he knows. Because we've built the relationship. I want him to know I'm there for the long haul. I'm there for when things are good, I'm there for when things are bad.

And I want to show him that I can be honest with him. Sometimes players just have to know that they stink. They have to know that what they're doing at this point just isn't quite good enough. It doesn't mean they're not capable of it, but sometimes the truth is, "You know what? Right now you need to get to work." I believe when you can show them that honesty, and there's a vulnerability there of the two of you trying to figure it out, it becomes a really good relationship. And if you have a really good relationship, I think you can change anything. I think you can do anything with that player. I think you can reach bigger and better heights.

That's the biggest and best piece of information anyone ever gave me.

Ron: My next question was going to be what advice you would give to a young coach who's where you were 25 years ago, just beginning a coaching career. I think you just answered that one as well.

Derek: Yes, and I don't think I could answer it any better.

Ron: I agree. So speaking of advice, what advice would you give a young pitcher? Maybe a kid who's finishing high school, or is in college, or is just getting started in the minors. What would you say to him?

Derek: I would tell him that the game is really hard. And for him to keep climbing levels, there has to be a resiliency there that's uncommon. To me, that's how a Major League player ends up separating himself. I think the majority of Major Leaguers have a resilience gene in them that is uncommon to most people. They've been willing to suffer more in some ways, and a lot of times, that's suffering on their own accord. Baseball can be a draining, exhausting experience as you climb levels.

Obviously in some cases there's a different talent level, but when I'm working with minor league pitchers I often tell them that they're throwing the exact same pitches as the guys in the big league. The difference is those guys make those pitches a little more often, and they're able to make them in a little tougher situation in a game. But in terms of the actual pitch itself, it's the same one. There are big league pitches being thrown in games all over the world, and at every level. The difference is the major leaguer can do it in front of a lot of people, in a really tough situation, and he can do it a little bit more often than the regular guy.

Ron: You talked earlier about a shift in pitching. The game of baseball itself goes through phases. We're in a period where everyone is knocking it out of the park or striking out. What do you think is the best thing that could happen in Major League Baseball in the next couple years?

Derek: I think the game is very cyclical, and I think it goes back into stages it's seen before. If you think about the root of baseball, it's the pitcher throwing a ball against the hitter and the hitter trying to hit it. That will always be the root of baseball. Everything else that happens around the game, happens from that. I look at it this way: Once hitters make adjustments, then pitchers make adjustments to that. Then once pitchers adjust, hitters adjust again. And so on. It's cyclical.

For example, currently throwing a ball up in the zone is a pretty big way of pitching. That's simply because hitters now are taught to hit the low pitch. 20 years ago you could throw the ball down and it was an out, because they were taught differently. I think you're always going to have the back and forth of that. That's why it's a great game. It's why people keep coming back to watch it. It's always going to be a series of adjustments between those two guys.

So I look for those kind of changes to happen. You're seeing the defensive shifts. The last couple years you've started to see players who understand how to beat the shift, and I think you'll see more of that. If that happens, then we'll adjust to it and not shift as much.

So for all the people that are trying to figure out ways of combating certain things, or imposing new rules, like no shifting, I think it will just be a matter of time before teams stop shifting on their own because of that. A lot of hitters are now thinking home run, walk or strikeout. I think we'll start to see more guys putting the ball in play. And we'll pitch differently because of that.

The strike zone has changed. Sometimes for the better and sometimes not. Look back to the 80s and 90s when some of the really great pitchers were pitching. Four or five inches off the plate was being called a strike. Now, it's a ball. If we start putting the ball in play a little bit more, we might start getting that call again.

It runs in cycles. There are always adjustments. It's always going to be strategic in nature. Because in the end, we're trying to win. So I think we're going to see a lot of different changes go back and forth. It's kind of like bellbottom jeans. They were really cool, then they were really not cool, and then they kind of became cool again. Baseball is the same.

Ron: Nice analogy. Last question, what's your favorite baseball movie?

Derek: *Bull Durham*. Maybe because that's the one I grew up with. That was the one that was popular. It came out when I was in high school. I just thought it was cool showing the life of a minor league player who had charisma, and was trying to help shepherd this pitcher that had a really good arm but really didn't know where it was going. I felt it was pretty authentic.

Ron: And as it turned out, you ended up shepherding young pitchers yourself. Thank you Derek, you shared a lot of great insights.

CHAPTER 6

WES JOHNSON

Wes Johnson is the pitching coach of the Minnesota Twins. He was named to that position in November 2018, coming from the college ranks. Wes became the first pitching coach in Major League history to  make the jump directly to the Major Leagues from the college ranks.

Wes spent nine seasons coaching at the college level. His last two years were at the University of Arkansas, which he helped guide to runner-up finish at the 2018 College World Series. Previously he helped lead Mississippi State to the SEC regular season title, and the NCAA Super Regionals.

During his college coaching career, Wes had 30 pitchers drafted by Major League teams.

Prior to coaching collegiately, Wes was a high school head coach in Arkansas, where his team won two consecutive state championships. He also coached American Legion ball, where 28 of his players signed an NCAA Letter of Intent.

Ron: Wes, your background in baseball is very deep and very wide. You've seen a lot of trends come and go since you began coaching at a small high school in Arkansas, then went on to four different colleges, and now to the Minnesota Twins. So talk about those trends, and how your experience at all these different levels helps you in what you're doing now.

Wes: It's interesting to look at the trends. Baseball used to be a very conventional game, where you just roll the balls out and take batting practice and throw the bullpen, and either you have it or you don't. Back in the mid-1990s we saw it slowly start to evolve. You'd see pitchers get more into weight training, and get stronger. I always wanted to develop players, so I never bought into the adage that you were either born with it or not. I'd say the biggest trend now is that we know power is developed, not something you're necessarily born with.

Ron: Let's talk a little about the different levels you've been at, and how you've seen things change going from high school to smaller colleges to major colleges to the major leagues.

Wes: I'm asked this question a lot. I always say, it's still baseball. You have guys come in who are good athletes, and they struggle with guidance and direction on how to use their talents. That's at every level.

Whatever level they're at, they also still struggle with the mental side of this. People think if a guy is in the big leagues, he's Superman. But a bad outing is a bad outing. The major leaguer has the same mental struggles as the high school kid who's a good player but goes 0 for 4 and thinks he can't hit now.

They're at different levels, and have different things to fall back on, but you still need to write development plans for each of these young men. I haven't seen a huge paradigm shift in what the player actually is, what you see when you peel the onion back. They still need guidance and direction on what to do with their talent. They still need an individual plan to help them get better. And they still struggle mentally at times with how good they really are.

Ron: I often refer to you as a constant learner and a lifetime student. How important do you think those characteristics are to young coaches that are trying to move up into higher levels of competitive baseball?

Wes: I always feel like somebody else is getting better than me if I'm not trying to learn today. The way the game is now, and keeps evolving, you're looking for the edge all the time. And if we're not out there searching for it, and searching for a better system and a better way to do things, then we're going to get in trouble.

That's so important for young coaches. Especially if they want to be able to do things at the next level. If they aren't waking up each day trying to learn, trying to refine their process on their own and not someone else's, they're just going to be average.

Ron: How influential have people like Brent Strom and Derek Johnson, who are also in this book, and Paul Nyman and Flint Wallace been to your development as a pitching coach and also a developer of young men?

Wes: I've said for a long time that the Texas Baseball Ranch was the center of the universe when it came to pitching. Not because you have all the answers, but when you get into a room with guys like that, not to mention Randy Sullivan, and of course, you, the things that start to happen and the ideas that result, are just priceless. I wouldn't be in this book without those people.

And it's not just pitching. The influence you have on young men not only affects them from a baseball standpoint, but also a life standpoint. It shows them what life is about. And to me, that's as big as anything we're doing with pitching.

Ron: That's a good point, because every year in the major league baseball draft, they're picking high school kids. And for every one that makes it to the majors, there are countless more who are going to work at it for years and then reach a point where they realize this is as far as they're going to go. Even the ones who make it big aren't going to get there overnight. They're going to go to college, they're going to go through the minor leagues, and they're going to struggle. However they end up, it's a development process. You've helped develop a lot of these young men. It's a long way between starting a baseball career and pitching in the Major Leagues.

Wes: I think back to when Brent Strom, at one of the boot camps we all used to work at, rolled out a growth mindset. He made it real simple. I don't know if it was his definition or someone else's, but it's a good one. He said, "Hey, that's just a belief that who you are today is not who you're going to be tomorrow."

You always talk about how important it is to not only work, but have a plan to do it, so you can have this growth mindset. And when that growth mindset hits, you see these young men start to transform. One of the things we're seeing today with young pitchers is they're so athletically gifted, but they get into professional baseball and start to struggle. If they're lucky and go to places like the Texas Baseball Ranch or the Florida Baseball Ranch, they start figuring out they need to have that growth mindset. So they're able to redial and continue to play the game. Unfortunately, for some of the other guys, that sand in the hourglass is almost empty.

Ron: What do you think are the biggest changes that have occurred in the training of pitchers while you've been in the trenches doing this every day? And how have those changes affected the game at the college and professional level?

Wes: I think the biggest change started when Paul Nyman rolled out with weighted ball training and the delivery. Then I look at how you were able to put that into a system for us to be able to use with players. And then the last piece of that would be individualized plans. I can't emphasize enough about assessments that are done on players and how we are able to take them and use them. While everybody's throwing a weighted ball now, they're doing it for different reasons. When you look at recovery and health and all of these different things that are important to a pitcher, being individualized is probably the biggest thing I see that has changed the game.

Ron: So now that we've looked back, and looked at what's going on now, let's take a look ahead. What do you predict will be the next big thing, or couple of things, that will evolve and improve over the next several years in professional baseball?

Wes: I see what's going on with Force Plate data right now. I had a Force Plate mound built a couple years ago, but we're only just now really understanding it. The biggest challenge we face right now is the ability to keep a young man healthy. Not only keep him healthy, but performing at a very, very high level. I think the Force Plate data is going to really help us figure out that recipe.

You're starting to see more and more major league teams take advantage of that. For example, the Twins use a biomechanical marker system on the field, so we can take that data and use it with a Force Plate. I think what's going to happen in the coming years when we really get comfortable with this, we're going to be able to maximize a guy's performance and also maximize how long we can keep him healthy and on the field.

Pitchers suffer from degeneration of muscles, and tears, and so forth. One of the things you do at the Ranch is work with them to pitch more efficiently, and put less strain on their body. When I get these young men, we may do a video analysis, or put them through assessment, and deem them clean, so to speak. I know there are many who have come to see you after the damage was done. You cleaned them up, but I hope they'll start going to you and Randy earlier, and get educated on the health and durability required in this game. That will be good for them and good for baseball.

Ron: You've presented a number of times at coaching clinics including the biggest one, the ABCA, the American Baseball Coaches Association. Share what you talk about, and what it means to you personally to present at events like that.

Wes: I try to talk about new things because you want to keep your material fresh, but in every talk I come back to mindset and how important it is to have the right one. I also hit health, how important it is for the athlete to be healthy. I also stress that we have to individualize. Don't just think you're going to buy this program from whoever and it's going to fit you and it's going to work for you. We know through much science and research that's not the case.

What does it mean to me? I'm always humbled, because quite frankly, "Holy cow, they want me to speak? I'm just this little old guy from Sherwood, Arkansas that loves the game of baseball. I'm nobody special." So I'm always extremely humbled, and quite frankly, blown away that people still want me to come speak.

Ron: Let me point out there are only 30 major league pitching coaches, and you're one of them, so you've reached the pinnacle and that is very special.

Speaking of events, you've been a big part of the Ultimate Pitching Coaches Boot Camp at the Ranch. Talk a little about that.

Wes: The coaching boot camp is the one that everything is modeled after now. What I love about it is it's almost like it's the center of the universe for pitching. Not that you're going to come there with all the answers, but a lot of the answers to whatever everybody is searching for will come out of that camp.

The speakers are phenomenal. But for me personally, it's what goes on after it's over at the end of the day. People gather, and we're talking about pelvic rotation, or body efficiency, or whatever we bring up. I can't tell you what it's done for me as a coach over the years. I wouldn't be where I am today without it.

And I believe the boot camps for pitchers are one of the best things any young pitcher can go through. When you walk out of there, you may be a very successful athlete and you may not have any pain, but we know this: In the game of baseball, you're going to have failure at some point, whether that's results, or an injury, whatever it may be. Attending those boot camps, helps you have a plan to attack all of those areas.

You may be fine right now, but we all go to the doctor for a checkup when we're fine. We take our kids to the doctor to make sure they're getting their shots and growing up healthy. Boot camp is like a checkup for these young men. Like I say, not everybody has an issue right now, they're healthy and they're having success, but just wait. It's coming. I don't know when, but it's coming. We've done this too long to not know that.

Ron: Speaking of young men, what advice would you give these young, aspiring professional pitchers? The ones who are, let's say, 16 to 22. What advice would you give them on their development path?

Wes: I think the biggest thing for that age group is that you'd better have a great training program, and you'd better understand how to have your arm ready for whatever season it is for you. If you're a multi-sport athlete, and you play football and basketball and baseball, you've got to know how to get your arm ready.

Once again, I think that's what the Ranch and Paul Nyman and everybody else who's associated with them has brought to the forefront. Know your workload and then have a plan to train your body to that workload. Instead of vice versa, where we say, "I'm going to go have this heavy workload, and then I'm going to rest, which will let me recover." We've found through science, that's not the case.

Ron: And what advice would you give to the young, aspiring coaches on their development path?

Wes: One of the things I've learned over the years, from the Ranch and all the people we talked about earlier, is "Don't be a Twitter coach." In other words, don't see something on Twitter or Facebook or anywhere online, and believe it's the be all and end all for every one of your players. There's a reason we're individualizing and we're having success with it. The challenge is, you have to be a constant learner, and you have to try to get to know each player on an individual level.

The other thing I would tell a lot of young coaches is we've lived in this baseball world for so long, where everybody thinks it's got to be so nice and neat. Everyone has to line up and do 15 jumping jacks together, and then everyone has to do the same stretching exercise, and then everyone has to do the same weighted ball exercises, because it's nice and neat and simple. And then we get done and everybody plays catch at this distance, and everybody throws the pen on Monday and Wednesday.

And what you find out is, the longer you do this, the furthest it is from the truth. There will be guys who need certain drills but don't need certain others. I think everyone wants the shortcut. Everyone wants the silver bullet. Well, there may be a few silver bullets, but major league baseball certainly banned one when they banned PED's.

Ron: What's the best advice you ever got during your coaching career?

Wes: Probably the best advice I got is, the more you learn, the more you're going to figure out you don't know. And that's the truth. It's like I tell my players all the time, I don't know everything, but by Gosh, we're going to find out. We'll figure it out. I'll research it until I can't research anymore and then we'll move on.

And that's the other thing I learned. You have to treat each player individually. Everybody's got a different personality. Everybody was raised differently in their household. It only makes sense for me to think we have to individualize.

Ron: One last question. What's your favorite baseball movie?

Wes: Oh my Gosh. I'm old school. I love *The Natural*.

Ron: Good answer. Wes Johnson, pitching coach of the Minnesota Twins, you have shared a lot of information that any young pitcher or pitching coach can benefit from.

IN THE

BULLPEN

CHAPTER 7

ADAM BARTA

Adam Barta is the founder of Blizzard Baseball Academy in Minnesota. Since it began in 2003, Adam and his program have graduated some of the most-decorated prep athletes in the state, as well as helped  develop youth players from ages six through 18.

In 2006, Adam joined the Chicago White Sox organization as an associate scout. His main duties are scouting players in the Twin Cities and running the Minnesota Area Code workouts. He has identified a number of players who were either signed or drafted by the White Sox.

Adam pitched in college and professionally, and coached at the collegiate level. He has given numerous coaching and pitching presentations, including at the Minnesota Baseball High School Convention and the Minnesota Twins Coaches Clinic, and has served as a consultant in pitching mechanics and arm care.

In 2016, he founded the JP4 Foundation (formerly the Blizzard Foundation), a non-profit organization that provides financial aid to student athletes in need, funds community service projects, and provides a college scholarship to graduating seniors.

Ron: Adam Barta is the owner of Blizzard Baseball Academy in Minnesota, where they do some amazing things with young players. He's a skilled pitching instructor, has been a college coach, and is a scout for the Chicago White Sox, so his baseball career is very deep and well rounded. Adam, let's start with how you and I first connected.

Adam: I first heard about you through one of my Blizzard players, Nick Juaire. He had been to the Texas Baseball Ranch for several years, and his mom told me I really had to meet you, because there was a lot of synergy between our programs. So I called you, we talked, and the rest is history. What you teach is similar to my philosophy, but we've both had to do a little adjusting.

Ron: Even though we both work with pitchers, we're not competitors, we're really more like partners.

Adam: Yes, I think we both begin with a relationship, and the teaching comes second. Your values, and the way you teach, are so similar to what we do that it became very easy to work with you. Your motivation is based on what's going to help kids, and that's what we're about. The pitching stuff really worked itself out very quickly after that first conversation.

Ron: Blizzard Baseball is known for its player development. Talk about your development of training systems for pitchers.

Adam: The foundation of our academy is pitching. It's our passion. We begin with player development, and then the by-product of that is our teams. Because of that, our pitching has seen a tremendous amount of success. Then on top of that, implementing your systems has been tremendous. It has given us a little more structure on how we teach our guys, step-by-step. We were already known as one of the better player development places in Minnesota, but using what you've taught us has improved us.

It's impacted our guys tremendously from both velocity standpoint and a health standpoint. They've learned more about taking care of their arms. For example, take a couple pitchers in our 2019 class. Will Frisch and Drew Gilbert were the number one and number two prospects in Minnesota, and our potential first-ever first round draft picks from the state. Both are committed to Oregon State. Needless to say, they're pretty talented, and a lot of that talent is based on their hard work, but using systems you've helped us put in place has made them even better. Another example is Sean Bernard, an Iowa commit and Ben Pederson, a Missouri commit. These kids were throwing 81-83 mph when they were 16 & 17, and now they're throwing 87-94.

Their velo has gone up, but what's also important is their ability to stay healthy has improved. I think a lot of people don't understand that when you look at the big picture, velocity is only a sliver of what's really important.

Ron: You talked about player development. What do you feel you do particularly well as a training facility?

Adam: I think there are a couple different things. I think we teach basic fundamentals incredibly well. We do a very good job with the mental approach and the pitching approach to hitters. I think if you asked some of our clients, their first answer would be developing off-speed pitches and change-ups. We really stress the importance of having a good delivery first. Next we want you to command your fastball. Then we stress throwing change-ups before you need to think about throwing a breaking ball. That's the progression all our pitchers have, and I think parents appreciate that because they don't want their kids throwing curve balls too early.

Going back to the mental approach, we spend a lot of time working on how to pitch to hitters and looking at what's next. What are you going to have to look out for and what adjustments are you going to have to make? It's always thinking ahead, so you're focused on the things you have to get done now but also looking at what you're working towards. These are the jumps you've made, and here's what's coming up next year and the following year. It's getting high school kids ready for college, and college grads ready for pro ball. You try to help the kids have a vision and then put a plan together. Plan your work. Work your plan.

It's not going to happen overnight. It's hard work to get where you want to be, and that doesn't get done in a day. It takes 18 months, and it takes a while to see improvement. So, having that plan in place is really important for the kids. I think having that long-term plan is probably a big piece of why we're successful because we're not providing a short-term, gimmicky thing.

Ron: Blizzard Baseball and Texas Baseball Ranch have been teaming up once a year for the last four years. Talk about that event, and how our partnership comes into play.

Adam: If you talk to our players and our parents, you'll find our February pitching camp is one of the most valuable and important events of the year. They get so much information in a three-day period of time. I'm not a big camp guy. This is the one camp we do each year that's three or four days in a row. In fact, it's hard to consider this a camp because it's so in-depth and it's so individualistic.

Everybody has a certain plan based on what they do well and what they don't do well. I didn't really know what to expect the first time you came up. I didn't know how you were going to teach it, and in what form. But I was really happy with how much the parents are involved on the front end of it. I think you knock down some preconceived barriers that both players and parents have about pitching and velocity and perceived limitations. You opened everybody's mind to, "Hey, you can do this. You can get to 90. You can get to whatever your next step is." There was a ton of value in what you bring to the table when you talk to our kids, in terms of what things they can control, their attitude and their effort, and preparing for that next step.

Ron: You mentioned parents there. You help develop elite baseball athletes. What would you say to a parent who is entertaining the idea of taking their son to the Texas Baseball Ranch?

Adam: I'd say it's like having an encyclopedia set in front of you. You're going to get so informed about what you thought, about your misconceptions about velocity and how pitching works. The information you take away is going to help you as a parent, and help you understand how to help your kid as well. When it comes to bang for your buck, there's nothing close to it.

Ron: You certainly have a diverse background, as a player and coach and scout. You've been involved in many different levels of baseball, including professionally. Talk about how that has helped you in what you do.

Adam: I remember my very first lesson as a very young instructor. When you first go into teaching, it's easy to take the very simple things for granted. You have the information in your head, but often you don't know how to communicate it. So for me, having a diverse background, it all starts with being able to communicate with a young player more than just mechanical jargon. The best piece of advice I ever received was to teach every player to learn how to be a really good coach. Which is great advice, because 99.8 percent of them aren't going to play baseball for a living.

As a scout, a big piece of what you do with kids is "projectability". Say it's a high school kid. What is his ability? Can he pitch professionally, and for a long time? A big piece of that is what tools he has, his mental make-up, what he doesn't have, and what can get him to where he wants to be. I use the information I've gotten from you as a part of that evaluation. Say the kid is throwing 89 but he doesn't use his lower half properly. If this kid could actually learn how to use his lower half, he could be a 95, 96 guy. It's so important to make an evaluation based on all the information you have.

I look at teaching as the ability to know when to communicate with players, not just blurting out all the information you have in your head. Pitching checkpoints can be very complicated. A teacher/coach/mentor needs to be incredibly informed, and have all this information. But while it's detailed and it's complicated, it's not rocket science, so if you know it and you're able to communicate it clearly, it can really impact a player.

You and your team communicate it in a way anyone can understand it. My 10-year old went to your camp last year, and he understood the analogies. Then at the same time, Will Frisch, who's a potential first rounder, was at the same camp, understanding the same things. It's not easy to have a young kid who doesn't have an idea about pitching, and a potential first rounder with a fairly good handle on what he's doing, both get something out of it. The way you teach has helped me to be a better teacher and a better communicator.

It's not just the mechanical part, the inspirational part is important. If you don't believe you can do it, you're not going to be able to do it. You have to get over that hurdle, to be able to say, "I can do this." If you believe in yourself, you can knock down some barriers you originally created for yourself. There's this self-realization for players when they put in hard work and they see results. It's what our academy is based on. Both the physical side and the mental side of pitching.

Ron: It may not be rocket science, but there's a lot of science in it. It's athletics based on scientific principles. It's science-based training. That's how we take that kid who's throwing 89 mph without using his lower body properly and make him a 95 mph pitcher.

Adam: 100%. It goes back to the teacher. I think the genius of a good teacher is having that knowledge within you, and knowing when not to say it, too. It's making sure how you communicate complicated things is simple.

Someone who does that well is Neil deGrasse Tyson, who's a real rocket scientist. When you listen to him talk, it seems simple. You think to yourself, "I can't comprehend what he knows, but what he just said makes sense," because of the way he communicates it. So you actually understand rocket science.

Pitching is very similar, in that the teacher has to be incredibly well informed to be able to figure out all these nuances, and how to communicate them to have the best impact. And it's not only what you say, but how you say it, the emotion in which you say it. Knowing that is the sign of a really good teacher.

Ron: You and I have had a front row seat to this training revolution in the past decade. Talk about the evolution of training.

Adam: I think 10 years ago we had a lot of hypotheses about why somebody throws hard or why kids are getting injured. It was easy to say, "You're throwing too much, so you're going to get hurt." That's true for some, but not for everyone, and it wasn't backed up with as much statistics or as much research. I believe there were a lot of so-called quick fixes implanted that didn't fix anything, but now, I believe what's revolutionized training is data driven, theory driven, and research driven results.

And let's face it, there's been a growth in the importance of velocity, because right or wrong, it's what's getting kids noticed, it's what's getting them scholarships, and it's what's getting them drafted.

Just the other night, I was watching the Yankees game, and there were 54 fastballs thrown. There wasn't a ball thrown under 96 miles an hour. So you have these people who are chasing velocity, and while some people can get you those numbers quickly, I think what you've done is brought something very important to the forefront. Yes, velocity is important, but there are a lot of other books on the shelf that are important as well. The velocity piece is one sliver of what makes a pitcher long standing.

So I think while you had quick fixes and unproven theories 10 years ago, I think now what you have is a breadth of knowledge. That's really what you bring to the table. You bring the velocity piece, but also, "Where are you at physically? Do you have a weak arm? Do you have a weak shoulder, weak elbow? Are you weak in the backside? How is that impacting your delivery, and then how is that impacting your velocity and command?" You have all these slivers of information and once you put those slivers together, you have this big oak tree.

Unfortunately, people look at the sliver, like how can they throw as hard as possible, when the first question they should be asking is, "Why does my elbow hurt?" So let's get that figured out first, then focus on keeping it healthy, and then we can focus on throwing hard. When people focus on that sliver it's dangerous because people get hurt.

You and I pay attention to all the slivers. The health piece, the nutrition piece, the velocity piece, the mechanical piece, all of the other pieces that separate a good athlete from a world-class athlete. I think people are paying attention and will continue to pay attention.

And it's not a cookie cutter process. While there are some absolutes, they have to work within everybody's uniqueness.

Ron: What do you see as the future for this type of training?

Adam: Honestly, I think we're already in the future. I'm not saying it's as far as it can go, but I think this trend will continue. I believe we're going to see a lot more data analytics based on the human movements, and how those movements can be manipulated and massaged and adjusted to get the maximum amount of effort from the human body. In order to do that, we're going to need more data and more research. It's going to become more analytical on how the human body works. That's why you're seeing spin rates, and exit velocity, and range factors, because those things have equaled wins at the major league level.

I wouldn't call that the next step, I'd call it the advanced step that's already out there.

Ron: Last question: as with any successful movement, there are going to be copycats and mimics. There are already other programs trying to imitate and replicate the training systems we use. There can be significant downsides and dangers to that. Talk to the parents and coaches reading this book. Tell them what they should be aware of when they're considering a program for their son or their athlete.

Adam: That's an easy question to answer. You need to talk to other people who have been a part of those systems. Talk to people who have been part of program X, Y and Z, and then talk to people who have been part of Texas Baseball Ranch or the Blizzard Academy. Ask what worked for them and why it worked for them. People from those copycat programs won't be able to answer that.

Then look at the people involved. The people are the foundation of everything. That is the backbone of the Texas Baseball Ranch. The ideas and how we teach mechanics are important, but the people behind it are every bit as important. When you have copycats, they're typically people who aren't innovators, and aren't creative, and aren't in it for the right reasons.

Those people come and go. You've stood the test of time. It's hard to do that in baseball, or any other realm, whether you're a violin player, a sales director or any profession. Those things are difficult. The people who last are the ones who are smart and innovative and creative and do it for the right reasons. It's not the ones who focus on what other people are doing. That's when you take your eye off the ball. I like to think we've never done that.

Ron: That's a perfect way to wrap up. Thank you Adam. You've shared some great insights and shown why you're so highly regarded as a pitching instructor.

To Adam Barta:
Phone: 612.790.4200
Email: abarta@minnesotabaseballacademy.com
Website: www.blizzardelitebaseball.com

CHAPTER 8

ALEX CREEL

Alex Creel is the head of the Golden Spikes pitching program, in the Sacramento, CA area. He has spent more than 3,000 hours of instruction helping kids of all ages improve velocity, location, and, most importantly, arm health.

His pitching program helped five pitchers break the 90 MPH barrier. Four of them were drafted by Major League teams.

As a player, Alex was highly recruited and ranked by Baseball America as the 49th best high school prospect in the nation in 1999. After arm injuries cut short his playing career, Alex turned to coaching and became a student of pitching mechanics. He is one of Northern California's preeminent experts on pitching mechanics, arm health and enhanced velocity.

Ron: Alex Creel is the co-owner of the Golden Spikes Baseball Academy and the owner of K3 Pitching in Northern California. After arm injuries cut his pitching career short, he set out to help others pitch better and stay healthy, and he's had a big impact on a lot of players.

Alex, anyone who's ever done a Google search will get a kick out of the way we originally met.

Alex: Yeah, it is pretty interesting how our paths crossed. I had been away from the game for a while after injuries ended my playing career. I learned that I was not meant to be stuck in a cubicle behind a desk and a computer. I decided to seek out what I have always been passionate about, which was baseball.

I was offered an opportunity to start coaching at a local HS and took the job as the Head Coach at El Camino HS. Shortly after, a local Academy hired me as their 11U coach and pitching instructor. It became my career and I wanted to make sure that I was offering information that would help players get better and achieve their dreams.

I was looking for some help in developing pitchers besides what I was taught when I played. I played for a lot of great pitching coaches in college like Fred Corral at SCC and Jerry Weinstein at Cal Poly. Since JW was the last person to have helped me, and we were training, using different methods to improve my performance than I have ever seen before, I decided to Google him and see what came about. Somehow you showed up in the search. That's how I learned about the Ultimate Pitching Coaches Boot Camp, and our relationship started from there.

Ron: Now, you and your facility, K3 Pitching, are known for player development. Talk a little bit about that.

Alex: There are a lot of ways that you can improve a player. I'm just trying to make sure that whatever level you're at when you come in, we're getting you better on the way out. At K3 Pitching and Golden Spikes, we are trying to help you in as many areas as we can. Whether it is your mental game, strength and conditioning, throwing plan, movement patterns, velocity or command, rest/hydration/nutrition, we are always striving to learn and improve our methods to further help our players.

Ron: Talk about some of the changes in your training systems since we've hooked up.

Alex: First off, the wake up/ warm ups that you have shown me have been huge for training our athletes. When I was younger, it was always "Jog to the fence, stand around the circle, and someone will lead a static stretch." You showed me how that doesn't really warm up the body to recruit the muscles that are going to be used while throwing a baseball. You made me aware that the body is only able to recruit muscles, if they have actively been warmed up. I saw what the Ranch does to get pitchers ready and it made sense to me. The dynamic stretch to get the body active, the tubing to get the trunk and arm ready to go, the Shoulder Tube to get the arm some blood flow, all these activities have really helped us come up with different routines to get our guys ready for battle. I wish I had this understanding before I became injured in HS. I did not know how to get ready like this nor did I understand the importance of preparing like this when I was younger.

I have gained a deeper understanding of what I should be looking for on video analysis and how to help the player reach his full potential. I am still trying to pull as much knowledge as I can from you and others, but I am much better at helping players than when I started. You introduced me to the Connection Ball and it has become a staple in our facility for teaching the upper half in the throwing process. The presentations that you have given at the UPCBC through the years on deceleration have shown me what to look for and how to fix it with different drills and tools. All these things have helped my players gain a better understanding and feel for what they are trying to do if we are working on disconnects or poor decel patterns.

Before coming to the seminars, I had no idea about energy systems that the body uses during physical activity. Most of baseball is played in a very short period of time. The explosiveness of a throw or a swing, both take place in under a second, yet many coaches are teaching players to train over a longer period of time. The ATP/CP energy system is the system that our body is using during the game of baseball. It is the initial burst of energy and can last for about 14 seconds. After learning that at the Ranch, we have designed our post throwing power workouts to stay within that time frame, so we are training to become faster and become the best at moving fast in that system. We believe it is a must do in order to gain velocity. You have to train the way that you would play. You've shown me a plethora of exercises that we use to help our players explode in the ATP/CP system.

Ron: Is there one thing you do exceptionally well as a training facility, or is it the overall process?

Alex: I think we are exceptional at building a bond with our students. We really care about how our athletes are doing in their day to day lives as well as how they are doing in baseball. We want them to feel cared for not only as a pitcher, but as a person. We know that some of the things that we set out for them to do in our training is difficult, and that there is going to be a lot of failure. We make sure to remind our students that challenging them past their current capabilities is the only way to grow.

Since we have built that foundation with the player, he feels more comfortable and confident putting himself in more vulnerable situations because he knows it is his way to success. He trusts that we are doing what's best for his development. He begins to accept more challenges and knows he has the support from us to help him in any way we can to grow into the pitcher he wants to be.

When personal records are beat or pain in their arm is not present in a throw like it use to be, we really try to work the myelination process by celebrating those moments with tons of emotion. Therefore, we are letting the body know that the movement just made was good, and we are speeding up the learning process. The kids that we train, really enjoy this and we are just as excited as they are for their achievement. That type of learning environment is fun and a lot of improvements and growth can be made at a faster rate.

Ron: You are considered an expert on pitching mechanics, and arm health. Obviously that hits home with you, since your own career was cut short with arm injury. It's an area you and I both spend a lot of time on, because after all, a pitcher won't ever be able to pitch better if an injury won't let him pitch at all.

Alex: You and Randy Sullivan have been huge influences in understanding pitching mechanics and arm care. Not only have you taught me about disconnections in the throw that could possibly hurt a pitcher, but you have also shown me creative ways to help the player learn a more efficient pattern to keep their arm healthy. Players that train with us receive a video analysis to see what opportunities they have to make their delivery more efficient. Before studying your work, I really did not know what to look for in a player's delivery. Now, I have a better understanding of what I should be seeking out in a player's video.

We start out with the pitcher's deceleration pattern. If we see problems in the video analysis of the way he finishes off a pitch, we know we need to fix his deceleration issues. We use a series of drills and instruments to help players learn the desired movement pattern. For example, using the throwing sock in drills gives your arm a little resistance after release, so you start going into pronation and rotation at the end of your throw, thus keeping the elbow loose and bent, which we think keeps the arm healthy. We believe that this will help the player with any pain that he might be experiencing in his posterior elbow or shoulder.

A few things that we are looking for at footplant are hand inside throwing elbow, elbow at or slightly below shoulder height, and if the glove arm scap is connected to the spine. If the player is showing any concern in the above areas, the Connection Ball, Bell Club, and Connector Club have really helped us get our players to feel what a more connected throwing arm or glove hand feels like. Again, after the diagnosis our prescription is to find the throwing drills that help the player choose a more efficient throw. The arm action drills that I have learned at the Ranch eliminate time, and when you eliminate time in the throw, the more efficient arm action begins to show up, especially if you are coupling the drill work with the use of the connection ball.

Lastly, we try to identify anything in the lower half that can be adjusted to help the player have fluid, full body throws. As the player goes into leg lift we would like to see the throwing side hip slide under the front hip and behind post leg heel as he is going into leg lift. That will help to start building direction towards home plate and the hip hinge that he is creating will help him to rotate off the rubber instead of push off the rubber. As the player nears the end of his pelvic load, he should continue to ride the back glute down the slope of the mound. Further loading of the glute will help the pitcher use the muscles that will rotate his lower half into foot plant. At the end of that riding down the mound action, we would like to see the player rotate his pelvis into footplant. I want to see the back leg initiate the arm being flipped up as the front foot is going into landing. If the throwing side hip is not rotated far enough into footplant, it makes it very difficult to release the ball out in front of the body, thus putting more stress on the shoulder and elbow. We use drills that you and Flint Wallace have taught us like "back leg rotators", "box squats", "hook 'ems", and "drop intos" to help the players gain a feel of how to create a more efficient lower half. We will try anything we can do to get that guy to feel that lower half working in the right sequence. Clear objectives for each drill are vital for the player to do the drills properly.

Once they start to get the drills down, we blend those segments back into their delivery. Blending is taking a drill or series of drills and doing them before he throws a pitch off the mound. After viewing the "Blending" DVD you released with Brent Strom, it really made me aware of how pitchers should work on a more efficient delivery while not really thinking about it as they stand on the rubber of the mound. The mound is reserved for making pitches, forcing contact, and getting guys out. Our players are being trained to stay true to being a fierce competitor on the mound by staying focused on the task at hand instead of becoming consumed by the "perfect" delivery.

Over the years of putting together what I have learned at the Ranch, this process that we have pieced together has been extremely helpful for our players' pitching mechanics.

Ron: This training is almost a revolution in baseball. Let's talk about how it's evolved, and what you see as the future for this type of training and player development.

Alex: Throwing a baseball with as much force as you can is not just mechanical, it's strength training as well, and what we're seeing is the way the body produces power is being misinterpreted. Your typical strength-training program for baseball players is to get into the weight room and lift heavy things to get stronger, which makes sense, but is that the way your body really needs to train to be "sport specific?" Yes, we need to get strong, but what type of strength training programs are going to give us the best return on the time we put in doing the work?

When Randy Sullivan presented at the UPCBC '17, he described some characteristics of functional baseball training. The strength-training program should demand the right energy system, have the appropriate types of movements, have a clear goal, and take muscle slack out naturally. Taking the slack out of your muscles was the one that stood out to me the most because I had no clue what that meant. Randy mentioned that there are 3 ways to take the slack out of a muscle to produce max force: 1) Make a counter move 2) Place heavy external loads on the body 3) Force Co-Contraction. Most strength training programs place external loads on the athlete. The problem is that will not take the slack out of the body naturally, so that type of training will not be available to a player in a game time situation. Players need to be able to take the slack out of the muscles quickly in their body in a game-time situation, so you have to create workout programs that have the player actually doing that.

The evolution of training using water bags creates instability from above forcing the body to go into co-contraction due to the unpredictability of the resistance. The player is forced to take the slack out quickly and the force development happens quickly, just like when a player is trying to throw a baseball to a target as hard as he can. I'm just starting to scratch the surface on using it with my guys, and have a lot more to learn on it, but if more and more trainers, colleges and coaches at the professional level are using this type of strength training for their players, it's pretty amazing to think of what the new age pitcher could possibly do.

Also, the evolution of how coaches actually coach is changing. Old school coaching is, "Let me tell you how to do it. Let me watch you do it. Here's what we could do better." Then repeat the process. In the past I have been guilty of this, and from time to time I still am. I need to constantly remind myself that's not how the body learns. The brain can hear that type of stuff, and the kid can be respectful and say, "Yeah coach I got it," but then he goes back to doing the same exact thing he did before. It's not because he's not trying, and it's not because he doesn't get it. It's because the coach isn't setting up an environment for these movements to start to happen.

What you have to do as a coach, is try to not just use verbal cues and talk the player through the movement you are trying to get him to perform. You have to try to actually get him to go into his body, instead of his mind, and get him to feel it. If you need him to get his lower half and hips right by sitting behind his heel as he goes into a glute load, just telling him to do that isn't going to yield the fastest results. You actually have to change the environment for him to make the proper movement. If there's a ramp or something you could put under his post leg to force his back hip to sit behind his heels, that's much better. You're getting the desired movement, so the body's learning the movement. You're talking to the body instead of saying it over and over to the brain.

Years ago, at one of your Ultimate Pitching Coaches Boot Camps, Frans Bosch said, "You have to talk to the body more. The message is too fast to throw a baseball for the brain to consciously tell the body what to do." Again, when we change the environment and allow for the student to feel the movement in their body, versus sending them verbal cues, we are speeding up the learning process.

The player universe is beginning to get better instruction on how to throw efficiently to stay healthy, how to strength train to enhance their on-field performance and receive coaching that not only speeds up the learning process, but actually gets them to make adjustments without cognitive thinking. It's pretty exciting to watch the evolution of this training and to think about where this game is going to be in the next few years.

Ron: I see you every year in December at our coaches' symposium held at the Texas Baseball Ranch. Talk about what you get out of attending this event annually.

Alex: There's something new every year. There are always new tidbits inside the drills that help make the drill more deliberate and gets the athlete to understand exactly what he is trying to perform. I also like the fact that The Ultimate Pitching Coaches Boot Camp comes in December. It ignites me! I come back home fired up and go into the upcoming year more focused and reenergized with some new training methods or drills to help my guys.

When I come back inspired, my kids feel that. We have new information to share with them that's going to improve their game even faster. The seminars go a lot deeper than just pitching mechanics and strength training. It's pretty neat that there are presenters that are not always talking about baseball, but ways to improve how humans learn and other concepts in life that can help you further assist your athletes to become the best they can be.

You get to see what is going on at the Ranch and how you continue to build your program to be the best it can be. You get to see what kind of culture the Ranch is building within their program and from there I am seeing what ideas I think I could implement into my program at home.

Ron: What we're all doing is having a pretty big influence on the throwing athlete, and baseball in general.

Alex: I love being a part of all the training involved and becoming a master coach in all realms of pitching and personal development. I enjoy finding a player's constraints on the mound and his body and helping design a program to get that player to where he needs to go. It's systematic and it's been a huge influence on a lot of people.

Look at the major leaguers who have come through your program, like Justin Verlander. Here's a guy who could throw 100 miles an hour but was struggling at one point when he played for the Detroit Tigers. After you helped him, he was throwing 95 to 100 again, was a playoff MVP and won a World Series.

Look at Scott Kazmir. He was out of baseball. You work with him and next thing you know he's hitting 99 MPH with Cleveland and signing a huge deal with the A's.

So it's not just working with young pitchers who want to make it to the big leagues. It's also working with athletes who have been there and are looking to regain what has been lost or for the next tier up in their development. When you find a player's constraints as a mover and a thrower, you can create a personalized throwing and workout plan that will improve the areas that are in need.

Ron: What do you think is the future of this type of training? How big can it get?

Alex: I think it should be spreading through all youth levels. This should be the standard of learning. And not just in the U.S. Nearly two thirds of Major Leaguers are Latin American. There are professional leagues all over the world. Imagine what pitchers would be capable of with the right training from a young age? If this information is well known all across the world, now we truly are making this game the best it can possibly be, despite where you are in the world.

Ron: When something succeeds, there will always be copycats. That's certainly the case with this type of training and these types of systems. What warning would you give to parents or coaches when they're considering a training facility for their son, for their athlete? How can they make sure they're making the right choice?

Alex: I would first want to know what the athletes do upon arrival when they join a new facility or coach?

        A parent should want that facility to go through a physical assessment trying to find their son's red flags first. At my place, like yours, we begin with a physical assessment and video analysis of the player's delivery. Once the red flags are discovered, there needs to be a plan of attack to correct the issues. Our physical therapist (Kirsten Carmichael of Next Level Performance) assigns them certain stretches or exercises to correct whatever constraints were found in that player's assessment. At least now you know you have an athlete that is ready for the physical demands placed on the body while trying to throw the baseball as hard and accurately as they can.

There are proper steps to go about throwing a baseball harder with more command. How can you start with solutions before you identify the issues? If you're not getting an assessment initially, that's a dangerous place to go. I'd want to know all those steps first. If you are truly looking for a way to help your son's needs, the training program must be tailored to him. Without that individualization, players are just receiving a "one size fits all program" that might not actually help him at all. In fact, it could actually hurt him. Everyone might have the same destination as their goal, but every person's starting point in development begins somewhere different. Finding a facility or coach that designs training programs around your son's individual needs is what I would seek out as a parent of a pitcher.

Ron: Last question. You work with elite young athletes. You were one yourself. You were a top 50 high school prospect. What would you say to any parent who is thinking about taking their kid to The Texas Baseball Ranch?

Alex: I would say this is an experience you will never forget. He'll get a lot out of it while he's there, and he'll learn what he needs to do when he gets back home. It's the way your program helps players from a holistic approach on how to throw a baseball better. You are always finding ways on how to improve what you do to develop players. Your training environment is second to none. A few of my students have experienced summer training or a 3 Day Boot Camp at the Ranch, and they have had nothing but great things to say about it. The Ranch's staff gives players a great understanding of what it is going to take to be the best pitcher he can be.

And, you train people to be better people. The culture that you have instilled at the Ranch teaches players how to lead and be resilient to what other people have to say. They are trained to not compare themselves to others, but to look inside and to compare themselves to yesterday's version of themselves. They are trained to stay in the game and continue to work towards their goal and never quit. Whether the player earns a college scholarship or makes it to the Major Leagues, or not, this type of mindset training will help players succeed wherever life takes them.

The Ranch becomes your lifestyle. They try to help your son understand that there are going to be problems in life. There are going to be struggles. There are going to be failures. Expect them, seek them, push yourself. That's where you learn, if you're willing to do the work and accept those challenges. That's where the growth happens. You need to embrace your own power, own your problems, versus seeking someone or something to come to the rescue. As you know, nobody can help you when you are struggling on the mound in the game. This style of training is preparing you to be able to handle all types of adversity.

I think these new paradigms can start in baseball and spread from there. Because if you've always been used to the coach who stands behind you, and watches you, and tells you how to do it better, then that process repeats itself over and over. That way of doing things will be extinct in the future. The new wave of players are self adjusters. They are mentally and physically prepared to handle pressure. The best players know that they need to constantly assess what their strengths and weaknesses are. They know how to create a plan going into their next practice to prepare for the next opportunity. They become their best coach. Those are the players that will succeed on and off the field.

Ron: Great point. Thank you Alex Creel, for sharing information any young pitcher or his parents can benefit from.

To Contact Alex Creel:
Phone: 916.847.1863
Email: alex@k3pitching.com
Website: www.goldenspikebaseball.net

CHAPTER 9

MIKE RYAN

Mike Ryan is the owner and director of baseball development and training at Fastball USA, just outside Chicago, where they specialize in velocity training, and are known for power development for both pitchers and position players.

Students come to Fastball from USA from across the U.S. and around the world, including Taiwan, China, Philippines and the Dominican Republic. In addition, Mike has conducted clinics in Taiwan.

He also spent 17 years as an associate scout for the Seattle Mariners.

Mike is the author of *The Pitcher's Code* and *Mike Ryan's Explosive Hitting*.

Ron: Mike Ryan is the founder of Fastball USA in Chicago, where they do amazing things when it comes to developing power for young baseball players of all positions.

I've worked with Mike for years. It's funny, when we first met in 2002 it had nothing to do with baseball training.

Mike: That's right, I actually attended one of your marketing seminars for Baseball Academy owners. You were a longtime Academy owner, and when you described some of the struggles you had faced along the way, I saw a lot of that happening within myself. At that point I was only about a year and a half into my Academy business.

Although I went there for marketing, I realized, "Hey, this guy has his stuff together when it comes to pitching," so I started following that. In fact, it's ironic you're interviewing me for a book, because you always joke I was one of the six or seven people who bought your first book.

Ron: Yes, we've come a long way. Now we've been working together for years, and for the last 10 years or so we've teamed up twice a year for an event.

Mike: Shortly after we met, you came out with the *Athletic Pitcher Program*, which was groundbreaking. But the problem was, it was so groundbreaking, not many people were doing it. So it wasn't a common thing in the baseball community. But I started implementing your work into our baseball academy. You and I held our first clinic together in 2004, and since 2009 we've been doing them twice a year. And they're working out great.

Twice a year, you come in with your staff and put on a clinic for not just our students, but students around the Midwest. You do thorough evaluations on each player, including physical evaluations and mechanical evaluations. You really look at their technique. Then you provide specific corrective exercises, tailored for each player. Each player leaves the camp with a plan, knowing exactly where they're at and what they need to work on to improve.

Ron: Fastball USA is well known for being progressive, and having cutting edge training. What you do, and what the Texas Baseball Ranch does, really work hand in hand.

Mike: That's correct. A lot of what we're doing in our training center in Chicago is very similar to the ranch style. We've adapted processes and thoughts. However, there are times I tell students they really need to work with you. If I had to trust one person to work with our guys, it would be you.

Ron: Thank you for that. Talk about some of the results you've gotten because of the training systems you've put in place.

Mike: As you know, I'm a big hitting guy. I've been able to apply a lot of your training processes and overall philosophies, not just with our throwers and our pitchers, but also with hitters. I've created what we call the *Explosive Hitting System*, which was impacted by a lot of your philosophies. So even though you work with pitchers, what you do also applies to hitting.

So, we help pitchers and position players. We work with them on their ability to hit the ball and the throwing end of it. We've been able to apply it to pitchers and catchers and infielders and outfielders, the whole team, the philosophy is important to all of them. In one training session, we will have outfielders, infielders, and pitchers, and we try to personalize the process each time.

Ron: Give me some of your success stories along the way. Talk about how you've helped some of these players and the results you've gotten with them.

Mike: Just to give you an example, we've now had three pitchers throw a baseball over 100 miles an hour, and 20 hitters go over 100 miles an hour with ball exit velocity. We've had another 181 guys go over 90 miles an hour, hitting and throwing combined.

Ron: That's very impressive. And the major leagues have noticed.

Mike: We've had nine guys drafted by major league teams in the last six years. None of them have made it to the big leagues yet, but you never know.

Ron: Speaking of young players, you have a teenage son who's a very good one. He has basically trained his whole life under these systems. How critical has this type of training been to him and his success?

Mike: Very critical. Jack made the national team at 12 years old. He's been playing high level baseball really his whole life. When my wife and I met you in October, 2002, she was pregnant with him, so he literally has grown up in your program.

For a guy his age, he's had great success. He's made a national team. He's already thrown a ball 90 miles an hour. He's hitting the ball 90 miles an hour. He moves well. But just as important as the physical side, it has definitely impacted his mindset. I think that's one of the undervalued things about your program. You're not just training the guys physically, you're working on what's going on from the neck up. I'm very proud of my son's approach, his training, his work ethic, and his ability to deal with success and failure.

Ron: You mentioned something you and I both think is very important. It's more than the physical aspect. It's more than positioning your arms and legs and hips. It's what's happening upstairs, the mental and emotional part of the equation.

Mike: It's important to help guys understand that where you are today, doesn't matter. It's about chipping away. We talk about one percent improvement. When you keep improving one percent here and one percent there, after three or four years, there's a big improvement. But I think the rest of the world gets stuck in labeling guys. They believe in what I call the prodigy theory. Someone is born to be great or they aren't. Yes, you need the talent, but the work ethic is so important. Once you have an honest evaluation of where you are, it's about chipping away and getting better, and improving. That's a mindset most people don't have. I think what you do really well is show guys what's possible. And you don't sugar coat it. You don't say it's going to be easy, but here's what's possible. People who get that, really do well in the program.

Ron: It's shifting the way you think, before you even pick up that baseball.

Mike: Exactly. I believe guys must understand why they're doing what they're doing, before they even do a drill or activity. It's absolutely critical for success. And again, you have to be honest with them. It can't be, "Rah-rah, you can do it." It has to be an honest evaluation of where you're at. You have to understand your weaknesses, as much as your strengths. And you have to buy in to the fact that it isn't going to be easy. If you don't have the work ethic, it's not going to work. That's where the mindset really comes in, because it's not easy.

Ron: These are interesting times for you. Your training systems are not only used here in the U.S., but you've taken them internationally as well.

Mike: What's happened is, people recognize that what we're doing is very different than most of the world. This past year, we actually did a clinic in Taiwan. When I went there, I knew I was going to bring them philosophies that went against a lot of things they were taught, and they grew up training with. So we needed to try to change their mindset and approach to training.

For example, my approach is hit the ball as hard as you can and as far as you can, where their approach might have been more contact oriented, or just put the ball in play. So we started with the mindset over there. It was a very successful clinic, and we hope to continue doing that in the future.

We're being noticed, and so are you. When we first started doing this, a lot of people looked at you like you were out of your mind. And now it seems we can't go a month without seeing you featured in something, whether it's Sports Illustrated or some other sports magazine, interviews on ESPN, or players and organizations seeking you out. They're seeking your advice. It's not so crazy anymore. They know you know what you're talking about.

Ron: As a training facility, what's the one thing you think you do exceptionally well? Whether it's hitters, fielders, pitchers, what stands out?

Mike: I would say, in a nutshell, we train players to become more explosive. In this day and age in baseball, to play at the higher levels, the guys who get first opportunity are guys who throw harder, move faster, and hit harder. Our specialty is really getting guys to tap into their natural potential of how hard they hit balls, how often they do it and how hard they throw the ball with accuracy. I think we specialize in, and do very well in, hitting harder, throwing faster, and moving faster. Overall, it's getting players to be more explosive with their movements.

Ron: Share a success story. Talk about a kid that came through your facility who was at one level when he started, but was a different player when he left.

Mike: On a higher end level, we had a player whose fastball was around 89 miles an hour. He played Division III college baseball. When I saw him throw, I realized he had a lot of potential, and I told him, "If you can get the ball up to about 95, you're going to change your life." In about a two year span, he took his fastball from 89 to 96. His throwing stats on the field went from 95 to 102. And he ended up getting drafted twice, out of a Division Three college program. He never made it to the majors, but he spent some time in the minor leagues, and he never would have had that without his spike in speed, which started with his mindset. He was the hardest thrower at his Division III school. But until me, no one nudged him and said, "Hey, you're pretty good, but I know you have a lot more in the tank."

Ron: Great story. You and I have both evolved a lot over the last 10 years.

Mike: The thing that jumps out to me is when your program first started, it was known as a velocity program. As the years have gone by, I've seen more of a holistic approach to training. It's not just velocity. It's command, it's arm health, it's mindset. It's an entire program. Velocity is just one portion of it, but it gets the most interest because velocity is exciting. It's sexy.

The second thing I've seen over the years is how you've learned how to personalize the system to each individual athlete, which I think is critical. You won't see too many people that are personalizing the system. You can go on the internet, and buy a velocity program, but it's not individualized to one player.

It can't be one size fits all. I can say from experience, it is a lot more work to individualize a program to an individual. It's one thing to have a system, it's another to have 30 different programs for 30 different guys. But it's definitely well worth it, and the students and the parents appreciate that, because they know they're working smarter, not just harder.

Ron: So where do you think it goes from here for this type of training?

Mike: I think we've seen one thing already affected. If you watch baseball, you see that guys are throwing harder than they've ever thrown, and the emphasis with hitting is now on exit velocity launching. People are starting to shift to where we were 10 years ago. Going forward, I think the big thing that's exciting is more people are getting the idea that these programs need to be individualized. In another five years, I think we're going to hear how everybody does individualized programs. You've already been doing that for years now.

Ron: That leads me to an interesting question. With any type of successful movement, there's going to be copycats and mimics. Some aren't going to be very good at it. They're going to be a knock-off of sorts. Are you concerned about parents bringing their kid to a program that isn't the original, that is trying to replicate something someone else is doing, but without the experience and the complete knowledge on why something is done in a specific way?

Mike: Yes, very much. To be honest, even here in Chicago, it's frustrating when I hear somebody say, "Oh, these people are doing what Fastball does", when I know that it's not even close to what we're doing. And there's a potential danger to this. Is it being personalized, or is it one size fits all? Because if people are trying to copycat, and they're not personalizing the program to each individual, they're putting these kids at risk of arm injury.

Let's be honest, not everybody is ready for a velocity program. But that's what I see advertised all the time. An academy will advertise an eight-week velocity program, and it's once a week for eight weeks. Well, that's ridiculous, because it takes a certain amount of time just to be ready for a velocity program. Those are all red flags to know they're just copycatting, and imitating, and trying to sell. It could be dangerous in the long run.

Ron: Speaking of moving ahead, you and I are expanding the Khaos™ Training. First of all, define Khaos™ Training, and then talk about how it's growing.

Mike: Simply put, chaos would mean that the hitter is put in an environment in which he has to solve problems. The training is never stale, and there's always a challenge, a problem to figure out. For example, if I throw batting practice to you, and I was throwing you pitches that were above your head, that's chaos.

If one pitch was above your head and the next was down at your feet, that's chaos. One pitch is way in, the next is out, that's chaos. Getting away from a stale training environment. In hitting, a lot of guys today will just put a ball on the tee, right down the middle and say, "Okay, hit it," and then in a game, they can't hit.

Or you've got somebody sitting in a chair throwing batting practice.

Our goal with some of the Khaos™ Training is to be able to throw different challenges at the hitter, for him to figure out. Khaos™ Training involves multiple levels of chaos.

For example, batting practice in which the ball is being thrown from multiple different angles at the hitter. It's basically making sure that practice is much harder, in order to prepare the guys for the game. Where most people are making the practice so easy, the game gets really hard. You can't have a stale training environment. It has to be constantly challenging.

There are multiple levels of Khaos™ Training so we can challenge the hitter slightly beyond their current ability level.   We don't' want to overwhelm the athlete either.

I look at it like we have multiple levels, almost like a video game. We are altering the environment in order to challenge the athlete to adjust and figure out how to succeed.   In most instruction, the coach is talking too much and trying to verbally instruct.   In Khaos™, we alter the environment and let natural learning take place.

Ron: You're the parent of an elite athlete. What would you say to the parent of a pitcher who is entertaining the idea of taking their son to the Texas Baseball Ranch?

Mike: I'll start off with this. It will be the best decision they've ever made. But I would caution them, they still have to be able to apply it. What they learn at The Ranch is incredible, but they have to have the work ethic to be able to put it into play. Because it's not a magic potion. It's not lightning in a bottle. It is great information, but great information doesn't work unless you work.

So, the program is awesome, but if your son doesn't have the motivation and the mindset, the work ethic to apply it, then he's wasting his time. You have to put the work behind it. And not just the physical work, the mental work as well.

Ron: Thank you Mike, for sharing your insights. And thank you for your partnership with the Texas Baseball Ranch. I can't imagine not being affiliated with Fastball USA.

Mike: I can't either. I'd be simply teaching what I was taught. I have all the respect in the world for the coaches that taught me, but I'd be stuck at being very average. I think one of the things that's been so important and beneficial is we've been able to prove and show our results on a daily basis. This system benefits the players, but also the business. It's a lot of work, but it's very motivating. I think it would be very difficult to keep the business open, if I wasn't following this kind of system.

Ron: Thank you very much, Mike Ryan of Fastball USA in Chicago.

To Contact Mike Ryan:
Phone: 224.209.7427
Email: fasballusa@hotmail.com
Website: www.fastballusa.com

CHAPTER 10

RANDY SULLIVAN

Randy Sullivan, M.P.T., C.S.C.S. is an arm pain expert and the CEO of the Florida Baseball Ranch® in Lakeland, FL, known for its world class processes for managing arm pain, reducing injury risk, and rehabilitating injured throwing athletes.

Randy has worked with pitchers such as Justin Verlander, Jake Odorizzi and Chien-Ming Wang. 19 Major League teams have incorporated the Florida Baseball Ranch's motor learning science into their pitching and hitting player development processes.

More than 270 of the Florida Baseball Ranch's students have topped the 90 mph barrier. FBR students signed more than $14 million in signing bonuses in just the last three Major League drafts.

Randy is the author of several books on baseball training, including *Savage Training, Start With The Pain,* and *Scaptivation: Bulletproofing The Next Generation of Elite Power Arms.*

Ron: Randy Sullivan is the owner of the Florida Baseball Ranch, which is known around the world for its elite pitching and hitting training, and he took a really interesting path to get there. Randy, before we talk about that, let's start with how you and I met, because I think parents reading this book will be able to relate to that.

Randy: As you know, I was the father of a 17-year-old left-handed pitcher who topped out at about 80 miles an hour. He was a very good pitcher, but at that speed he could never play college ball, which was his dream. I realized we had to help him learn to throw harder. But all the baseball traditionalists told me that was impossible, it was just a gift from God and trying to throw harder would be like trying to grow a bigger head.

At the time, I was in a career as a physical therapist. I thought, "This is just human movement. It can be taught. I may not be able to make him elite, but I can certainly help him improve." So I started doing some research. I found you online, and your stuff made sense to me, so I ordered your book. We began implementing the things you showed us, and began seeing some pretty good results.

And then we decided to come to Texas to work with you in person. It was one of those epiphany moments that changed everything. It evolved into a relationship and partnership that have blossomed over the years. You've been a mentor to me, and all three of my sons have trained with you. I tell people, "We went there looking for a better fastball, and we found a better way of life."

Ron: That's a wonderful thing to say, I really appreciate that.

Randy: I thought I would be running my physical therapy practice for the rest of my life, which would have been fine, but as we learned more and more about how to help guys throw harder, it also became clear that helping them stay safe and healthy involved the same variables.

Then my practice began to attract injured baseball players, because I was coaching in the baseball community, had developed relationships there, and they knew I was a physical therapist. So as guys overcame some catastrophic arm injuries, but also improved in ability, word got around and before long, my physical therapy practice was overwhelmed with baseball players.

Ron: There's a strong correlation between my processes and what you did as a physical therapist. It involves science, and working with players on how they use their bodies and how they move. In many ways, what you do now actually came naturally to you.

Randy: It's almost embarrassing that I was a physical therapist and a baseball coach for 15 years before I met you, and it never occurred to me that those two things would come together. But when we started talking and learning, I realized, "Wow, this is teaching human movement. This is what we do all day long."

That sent me on a feverish path of research that led to this collection of information from multiple disciplines. We began to study anatomy, physiology, biology, sociology, psychology, and neurology. I got into motor learning theory. That led me down to dynamic systems theory, which is based in differential calculus, so we had to hire a mathematician here to help us decipher all that. We've gone deeper and deeper into the science of teaching people how to perform the skill, and it's been phenomenal. The results have been unbelievable.

In the beginning, I think you and I were both considered heretics and radicals, and this was crazy stuff because it was so outside the box. It was different from what traditional baseball was doing. We both realized the traditional stuff wasn't working, so we had to start looking elsewhere.

We basically started wandering into these different disciplines and seeing what we could gather from each one. Somewhere along the line, I developed this knack for taking ideas from different places and merging them or synthesizing them into a process we could use.

You really inspired me to do that. I think about all the different dads who have been through the Texas Baseball Ranch, who had ideas and approached you with them. For you to take an interest in me and see that there was more there than what was on the surface, that there was an opportunity to build something really special, it really means a lot to me.

You encouraged me to continue with my self-improvement and continue growing, but in addition to guiding me through the process of research and development, you also helped me down the path on the business aspect. I think we make a pretty good team, and we get to help a lot of people while we do it.

Ron: It's all about helping players. Talk a little more about how you transitioned from rehab and therapy to training, and how you became the Florida Baseball Ranch.

Randy: We would see players with throwing injuries in our physical therapy practice. Their insurance companies would stop paying as soon as they were healthy enough to do things like raise their hand over their head, in other words, basic functional activities of daily living. Needless to say insurance wouldn't pay for them to get back to throwing baseballs, which is what they really wanted to do.

Historically, as a physical therapist, you would rehab these guys and then send them out with a traditional one-size-fits-all training program. And six weeks later, they're back with the same injury. But as I did research, and saw where your stuff was taking me, I realized there are reasons these guys are hurt. If all we do is rest and do traditional physical therapy, we haven't addressed the underlying issues. We didn't change the way they were throwing, so we couldn't expect them to be any better.

So we began to take these guys out and use your approach to teach them how to throw differently. I would pack up equipment in the back of my truck and drive around to Little League parks and work with them there. We found that their movement patterns changed. Their pain went away. Their performance improved. At first there were three guys. Then three became six, and six became 10, and next thing you know 25 guys are meeting me at a Little League park.

I couldn't do it like that anymore. Plus, we had started charging a fee for it, and you can't use county property to run a business. At the time, our physical therapy practice was in a little strip mall. We had two separate units, one for our practice and one for our administrative office. The pizza place next to us went out of business, so we expanded into that space to accommodate all these new guys we were getting. Then we moved our admin people into our main space, so the admin office was empty. We had it leased for another year, so we needed to use it for something. It was a long and narrow space, 15 by 60 feet. I looked at it and the lightbulb lit up over my head; a throwing facility! We built up the end wall with plywood, and after our patients finished physical therapy, we'd take them down there and they'd begin the throwing process. We called it the ARMory.

But soon we outgrew that space too. We were getting more and more popular. There was an acupuncturist in the office next to us, and he moved out because we were pretty loud. So we took over his space. Then we expanded into the back parking lot, but we kept growing, and we were bursting at the seams again. That's when our partnership began.

You saw how having the medical side added some depth to the process, and you said, "Why don't we form this thing called the Florida Baseball Ranch? If anyone gets hurt in our entire consortium, we'll send them to you for performance-based things in the southeast region." The nice thing about the arrangement is we both operate independently, but under the same general philosophy. Because we get together frequently, we're able to cross-pollinate new ideas. It allows us to get better, and help a lot more kids get better too.

Ron: The medical side is important. That's why I've always called you "the Mayo Clinic of arm injuries."

Randy: Thank you. That's pretty humbling. Along the way, I had written a book about how to manage arm pain and with your permission, I used your ideas. You had created an insightful list of types of contributors to subpar performance, and I saw that the same variables would contribute to pain.

You saw that the guys you were sending to us were getting healthy. You sent us some really high-end guys, like Chien-Ming Wang, who was out of the game after a devastating injury. He was throwing 80 miles an hour when he got here, and was at 97 by the time he left. He made it back to the big leagues. So the process was really working.

Many people have told me you called us the best in the world at helping guys overcome arm pain. That's not just flattering, knowing that you think we're that good at this has given us more confidence to keep digging deeper and deeper. We've really forged into performance-based stuff and motor learning theory.

As you know, we recently had our Baseball Skills Acquisition Summit. We'd taken this deep dive into the branch of neuroscience called motor learning and skill acquisition, which is how people learn, improve and refine movement skills? We took that information and applied it to baseball. We got together with a colleague in the Dutch national baseball program, and we put on the summit here at the Florida Baseball Ranch. It was basically how to use the science of skill acquisition and motor learning to enhance training for baseball players.

More than 150 coaches were there. 15 major league teams sent 53 representatives to come and learn from us about how to teach players how to play baseball, which was just mind boggling to me. It was really special to see how people appreciated what we were coming up with.

It's been incredible to watch the gains we've made, especially in the last five to seven years, once we dug deeper into not just what to train, but how to make the best of your training time. 10 years ago, we were radicals and heretics, and now Major League Baseball is coming to us. It's so exciting to be able to talk to people in major league organizations, and college organizations, and be able to share our ideas with them and help these guys get to that level.

But really, the credit goes to the players and the parents who invested in us and trusted us and allowed us the privilege of working with their kids. Those kids got better. They got so good that they started ascending to the highest level of the game, and they pretty much kicked that door down for us.

Ron: I firmly believe your skills acquisitions summit may actually prove to be a catalyst to change the way that athletes are trained in the future.

Randy: Based on the feedback we got, and the results we're getting, I think it's a huge leap forward. But you deserve a lot of credit for that, because you introduced me to the concept at one of your boot camps.

You had met a guy in Belgium named Frans Bosch, who had great knowledge of dynamic systems theory. It wasn't cheap to get him, but you paid his way and brought him to your Ultimate Pitching Coaches Boot Camp at the Texas Baseball Ranch. So here's Frans, this diminutive Dutch guy who's barely five feet four, and who knows nothing about baseball, standing in front of 200 baseball coaches telling them everything they've done wrong, and how to do it better.

The very first thing he said was, "The body shows remarkably little interest in what the coach has to say." You could have heard a pin drop in the room. Then he expounded on the theories of dynamic systems theory, differential learning and the constraints-led approach that we use today, and it was a revelation for me. It sparked us to start really digging into the research on how the people learn.

So yes, I do think it will prove to be a catalyst. We're already being contacted constantly by Major League teams, Major League players, and Little League players that understand that the new edge is in the how. Back when I played, knowing what to work on was a difficult thing. We all wanted to work hard, but we didn't know what to work on. I remember going into my mom's backyard and hitting an elm tree with a wooden bat a thousand times a day. I didn't get any better at hitting a baseball, but I got really good at hitting a tree.

But now, we have all this technology that has emerged. We have HitTrax and FlightScope and Motus and Rapsodo and all these technical advances that allow us to now assess and determine what it is we need to work on. Finding out what to work on has never been easier. The new frontier is, "How do I most rapidly and most efficiently and most effectively acquire that skill that I need to change?" That is where the science of motor learning and skill acquisition comes in.

I was thrilled to be able to connect all the dots, taking people from a lot of different disciplines and putting them together. Our mission in that summit was to let the scientists lay out the science, and then you and I were to be the bridge between the science and the application. We could interpret for the coaches, and say, "Okay, this is what this means." It really was incredible. It was the first-ever event of its kind, and already people are begging to know when the next one is and what we're going to do.

Ron: I want to follow up on two things you talked about in that answer. First of all, you mentioned Dutch baseball and you mentioned Chien-Ming Wang. What we're doing has gotten international attention, it hasn't just taken off here in the U.S.

Randy: Isn't that weird? It's amazing that I was just kind of grinding it out as a physical therapist for so many years, and then about four years ago, my business partner, Amy, who is the business mind behind our physical therapy practices and the Florida Baseball Ranch, pretty much fired me from the clinic. She said, "You can't be in here anymore. You're too valuable out there at the ranch."

It has just blossomed into this thing where I'm traveling around the world. The Chien-Ming Wang thing has sparked a whole flurry of interest for us in Taiwan. We're flying over there for the second consecutive year to work with their professional players and high school players on throwing. This time, they're inviting us to do hitting as well. I'm traveling to Italy. I've been to the Netherlands. I'm going to go on a trip to Canada soon. I can't believe that this game that I started playing when I was five years old has afforded me so many experiences that can't ever be replaced.

My kids are grown now, so I have all this time. It's great to have something to inspire you in this last quarter of your life to make a difference, with people, in life, and especially in the game of baseball. Of course, it's fine to have all that information, but if it doesn't work, if you don't produce results, then it's nothing.

Ron: The other part I wanted to follow is the technology and the technical advances. You've talked about how this type of training has evolved over the past decade. Now talk a little about what you see as its future.

Randy: This explosion in technology has really changed things. Now, instead of saying, "Hey, that ball moved pretty well," you have definable metrics telling you exactly what they're doing. You have data. And you can use that information to help identify strengths and weaknesses, but also use it as feedback to guide the training, to help him understand.

Now the baseball industry has migrated toward everything being science-based and data driven, which is fantastic. But I think the industry is making a mistake in thinking that the problems in throwing, the performance problems, the challenges we have in teaching guys to throw harder, have better stuff, be more dominating on the field, and the health and safety and durability issues will be solved through the scientific method.

The scientific method by nature is good. I love science, and we conduct scientific studies using the scientific method. But the scientific method hates variability. It tries to control variables. It says, "Okay, if I manipulate this variable and keep everything else controlled, and then I get an outcome, then I can pretty much establish a cause and effect relationship or at least a correlation or some sort of linear relationship between these two things."

For example, I did this training modality, and I got hurt. Or, I did this training modality, and I threw the ball harder. Or, I threw this many pitches, and I got hurt. Or, I threw this many innings and I didn't rest in the off season, and I got hurt. The problem is in complex systems, things like ecological systems, environmental systems, political systems, weather patterns, and the complexity of the biological system that is the human body, you're just not going to find linear relationships because all those systems are really complex.

By complex, we mean they have this infinite soup of variability. The current state and behavior of any one component at any given time is dependent on the state and behavior of the cell beside it, and so on, and so on. As soon as the variables start to interact and interfere and influence one another, the scientific method crumbles. So you have to go a little deeper. You can't solve it strictly with science. Our best hope is to combine a lot of different disciplines. You have to understand anatomy. You have to understand physiology. You have to understand the biology of the human body. You have to understand the medical science. You have to have at least a working understanding of the science of skill acquisition and motor learning.

Then, you have to take all that and apply it under what we call the dynamic systems theory, which really is based in differential calculus. Basically what it says is when you start running variables through these equations, they're going to form in predictable patterns. For that reason, we had to hire a full-time mathematician here at the Florida Baseball Ranch.

We have a guy that sits in the corner and calculates the numbers that we put together, and puts them through these equations and helps us use dynamic systems theory or dynamic patterns science by using his math skills to help us guide training protocols and help us guide our individualization of everybody's training. It gets really complex.

Ron: Again, that's why I refer to you as the Mayo Clinic of arm injuries.

Randy: I like that. But here's the thing. You still have to look through that science. You have to look through the prism of experience and common sense. Both of us have seen a lot of players play, and both of us have been around baseball forever, so we're able to take all that scientific stuff and whittle it down. At the end of the day, our job is to be a teacher, to teach people how to play baseball better. To do that requires something that a lot of training places and a lot of coaches leave out of the equation, and that is a relationship.

You have to build a relationship with a player. We know, based on our experience, that he doesn't have to know all the gears that are going on underneath the system. He doesn't need to know that we use dynamic systems theory, and we calculated his stuff. We can share that with him, but he doesn't care. He just wants to know what he has to do to get better. So what you have to do is build a relationship with each player. You have to understand who he is and what's going to make him work, and how we can design a training experience that encourages his body to choose the most efficient pathways of movement, and discourages him from choosing ones that are less efficient or less effective.

To do that, you have to be really creative in your design process, and you have to know your guy. You have to continue to know your guy and know when something isn't going to be good for him, or he won't like it. Because training is really about being a teacher. And being a teacher is about finding out how to meet your student where he is and help him become a better version of himself. So while you have to dig in to all the science, and understand all of it, in the end you have to be a master teacher.

Ron: Speaking of teaching, what would you say to a coach or an academy owner who is thinking about visiting the Texas Baseball Ranch and getting involved with this type of philosophy and this process of training?

Randy: I would quote you. You always say, "If you continue to do what you've always done, you're always going to get what you always have gotten." So if you're not happy with the results you're getting, or if you have a growth mindset that says "there's got to be more out there, there's got to be a better way," or if you're passionate about helping young men and women achieve their goals, then that's the place to be. This is a really effective blend of science, common sense, and interpersonal relationships and motivation of players that is unparalleled. I've never seen anything like it.

Every player wants to get better, but everyone has something limiting them from ascending to the next level. We're going to help you find that. We're going to help you figure out what you need to work on, and then we're going to help you achieve it in the best manner possible. Whether it's a coach, an academy owner, or a player, I would tell them this: Everybody has 86,400 seconds in every single day. Whether you play for the Los Angeles Dodgers, the New York Mets, the University of Arkansas, or the Himalayan Institute of Technology. It doesn't matter. Wherever you are, you get 86,400 seconds in every day. So if you're going to be better than the guy across the field from you,

you have to make sure that your training gets more out of your 86,400 seconds than he gets out of his.

To do that, you have to go to the people that are leading the world in optimizing training time, optimizing return on training time, and that's this Texas and Florida Baseball Ranch consortium. This is what we're doing, and so that's your edge. The new edge, the new frontier is how to get it done the best way possible, how to learn.

Ron: One last question. This is something you and I have talked about a lot. Anytime there's something successful, there will be copycats and mimics. What things do parents and coaches need to be aware of when considering what to do about training.

Randy: As you know, none of this information was ours originally. We took a lot of different ideas and put them together into this process that we use. We don't claim ownership of it at all. But if someone is trying to copy what The Ranch is doing, then you're copying what we were doing a year or two ago, and you're going to be way behind. We're always innovating and moving forward.

But here's what I would say to a parent. When I first started this, and I asked everybody I knew how to teach a kid to throw harder, there was zero information. The enemy for us was lack of information, so we had to go find and bring together all these different sources, and kind of forge our own way.

Fast forward to today and there's a velocity program on every corner. So for today's athlete, the enemy isn't lack of information, it's misinformation and disinformation, because there's this haze. All you have to do is throw the ball. All you have to do is lift heavy weights. All you have to do is long toss. All you have to do is these bands. All you have to do is this and that and the other thing. And they're all getting bombarded over social media and through marketing processes with all this information. What we see is, when clients come to us, they're confused. They need clarity. They need to know what they have to do to get their kid where he wants to be. Because they only get 86,400 seconds. You don't have time to go down the wrong path. You don't have time to do stuff that doesn't work, or gets your son hurt.

We've done this long enough that when parents come to our place, we present to them, "Here's how we view our role. Our role is to be your guide. Your son is the hero of this story, and we're there to shine a light on the path." But as we're walking toward the light that is success, whatever level that success is for him, there's danger in the woods. And if he goes off path, he could be in trouble. We view our role as walking along that path, shining the light, and saying, "Hey, when we're going down this road, don't step on those rocks. They have snakes in them. Don't eat those berries, they're poisonous. These are the ones that are safe to eat."

Our hope is that when we take a young man to that light that is his success level, he will someday come back and pay it forward and walk another person down that path. That's why, in our process here, we only hire employees who have trained with us. We don't hire from just outside because they just don't understand our culture, and they don't understand our process. These guys who are here all have the same passion because they lived it, and they felt it, and they did it. Their mission, their purpose in life, is to pay it forward and help someone else achieve the level of success that they achieved or even more. I don't think other places are going to tell you something like that.

Ron: That's a great way to wrap up. Thank you Randy. You shared some really worthwhile information. I'm grateful for our partnership.

To Contact Randy Sullivan:
Phone: 866.787.4533
Email: randy@floridabaseballranch.com
Website: www.floridabaseballranch.com

CHAPTER 11

JIM WAGNER

Jim Wagner is the founder of *Jim Wagner's Throwzone Academy* in Santa Clarita, CA, known for its commitment to arm health and recovery, and a throwing program that promotes a healthy arm with increased velocity.

Coach Wagner has worked with more than 10,000 players, including Trevor Bauer, an American League All-Star and Player of the Week during his time with the Cleveland Indians.

95 of his players have topped the 90 mph barrier and 20 have thrown 95mph or higher. 135 have played professional or collegiate baseball.

Jim is the author of *3 Strikes and You're Not Out*.

Ron: Jim Wagner is the founder of Throwzone Academy in Santa Clarita, CA. He's known for helping pitchers gain velocity while also focusing on keeping their arms healthy. He's worked with more than 10,000 players, so he's clearly doing something right. Jim, the way you and I first connected is an interesting story.

Jim: Yes, you never know what might happen when you go to a convention. I had just started doing pitching lessons, and happened to be helping a friend with his booth at the American Baseball Coaches Association's annual convention in San Diego. I was walking around, saw you, and we started talking.

But I already knew who you were, thanks to some old-school marketing. I had seen something in an old USA Today Baseball Weekly magazine, offering a curve ball report. I called the number listed, and got a copy. I had been working with a couple students, and I was disenchanted with the traditional pitching methodology, which was basically, "Get to Point A. Get to Point B. Get to Point C."

The curve ball report promoted one of your books, which I ended up buying. And everything in that book just seemed to line up perfectly with what I wanted to do with my pitchers, which was to be more athletic and more explosive. Your material really resonated with me.

So I talked with you for quite a while. In fact, when I got back to my friend's booth he was annoyed with me being gone so long. But throughout the convention I kept coming back to your booth, and we kept talking. You and I were really on the same page about a lot of things. I ended up bringing my son to one of your camps. Then we just started together, and it turned into a business association that's still going on strong after 15 years.

Ron: Your facility, ThrowZone Academy, is known for its progressive and cutting-edge training. Talk a little about the development of your training systems.

Jim: First let me say, you've been the most influential person in my business. Some of the things I learned from you include being athletic, being explosive, and doing drills that are a little bit more nontraditional. A number of aspects of how we run our classes are based on what you do at your camps and summer training. Obviously we can't do things to the same extent, because we're indoors in a limited space and you're outdoors on 22 acres. But you set the tone for the functionality of our program, doing different things at the right time, doing a lot of strength conditioning before we start throwing.

You also introduced me to weighted balls and the function of using them, not just in terms of velocity, but also in terms of arm health and arm care. Most people look at weighted balls as being potentially dangerous, but it's relative to the situation. Going for a walk is good for you, but walking on a freeway during rush hour is not such a good idea. We utilize our weighted ball routine based on what we learned from the Texas Baseball Ranch, and we continue to change things based on what you're doing.

There are a number of us doing this now, myself, Randy Sullivan at the Florida Baseball Ranch and Mike Ryan at Fastball USA to name a few. It all began with looking for better answers to some of the questions that were out there.

Ron: You have a pretty substantial training facility. Talk about what you do exceptionally well.

Jim: Number one, we are very good at getting players back being healthy. Players come to us who are hurting; their elbow, their shoulder, what have you. Over the last decade, we've sort of become known as the place where guys go if they're hurt, to get back to a healthy state.

The other important thing is we create velocity for players, and we do that in a safe manner. There are always people who tell you they're going to make you throw harder, but they come and they go. We've been doing it for a long time. There have been competitors that don't stick around because they just do the same old thing. We always mix things up. We don't do things the same way every single time a student comes in, even warmups. We have four different warmup routines. So we change it up, always while teaching players how to throw harder while maintaining arm health.

Ron: Speaking of the students you've worked with, I often tell people this story, which is a testament to your integrity.

At the time you were working with Trevor Bauer, who was clearly your best student. Instead of keeping him to yourself, you actually encouraged him to come to the Texas Baseball Ranch. Talk about your thought process, because that's not something a lot of people would do.

Jim: When I first started out, the first person I approached was Trevor's dad, Warren. Our sons were on the same travel team. Trevor was around 10 at the time. He was playing in an all-star game, and I walked up and said, "Hey Warren, I think I'm going to do some pitching lessons, and I'd like to work with Trevor." They agreed. So we started to do some work, and they really liked what they saw.

I had taken my son to one of your Elite Pitchers Boot Camps, and was very impressed with how you operated during that camp. One of the unique things about Trevor, other than his skills of course, is that he's always been a very progressive thinker. Working with him, we had changed some of the traditional things he was doing. I felt he would really benefit from your program, so I told his dad about it, and they signed up for a six-camp package. Trevor just fell in love with the place. Next thing you know he practically lived there for a summer.

You really challenged his mindset in ways I couldn't at the time, and the benefits to him were tremendous. I think you can argue that even though he was so skilled, he might not have progressed to the level he's reached if it weren't for the training he got in Houston.

Ron: That's a great story. Trevor actually stayed at our house a portion of several summers. You and I have now teamed up on an Elite Pitchers Boot Camp for a number of years. Share your perspective on it.

Jim: It's the West Coast version of the camp. One summer, I was in Houston with my son, who was training at The Ranch. Trevor was also there. At that time, you hadn't started going to different places for events. You and I happened to both be at the same gas station filling our tanks. You turned to me and said we should do something in California. I said that sounded good. I figured we'd talk about it at some point. But you said, "I'm serious, let's get this started." So we did.

We've now held them for 11 years and we're still going strong. It's called the Southern California Elite Pitchers Boot Camp, and it's evolved quite a bit from when it started. In the beginning, we used the first place where I worked, a local batting cage. I think people came just to hit. You said, "We need to be somewhere else next year." So we moved around a little, but now we've come up with a winner. We begin at my facility, then move to a local high school. We've also expanded it. It started as Friday through Sunday, and then we added a coaching clinic on Thursday night.

We get great reviews. Players get a ton of benefits out of it. The number of kids attending has grown, and we've built really good relationships with them. And it's working out for you as well, because it's become one of your bigger locations outside Texas.

Ron: I'm at your facility every year, and you're at the Texas Ranch just as often, if not more so. You attend many of our clinics, camps and symposiums. How have those events, and what you've done in Texas, translated into your own growth as a trainer and in your business?

Jim: Since 2003, I've been to every Ultimate Pitching Coaches' Boot Camp. Those coaching clinics have been absolutely instrumental for me in the development of my business. Coaches present new training ideas, new mindsets, and a variety of new developments. Plus, since I'm also a high school coach with a pitching staff, this has benefited me in terms of talking to my pitchers, trying to simplify things, and not getting too mechanical.

There's always so much to learn. The speakers include people from the professional ranks, the college ranks, and the high school ranks. I remember the first few years I was feverishly writing notes and trying to install everything I learned. Now I try to find four or five things that I hone in on, bring home with me, and incorporate into our classes. When I do, you can count on the kids saying, "Ah, we're doing something new. That means Wagner went to a coaching clinic." But again, we don't want to do the same things over and over. New ideas lead to a new way of doing things.

Another big benefit is the networking. That part can be very exciting. You and I happen to be doing this interview in the middle of the Cleveland-Houston playoff series. Houston's pitching coach, Brent Strom, has been a fixture with The Ranch, and has been a very good friend of mine for over a decade now.

Last year that friendship paid an unexpected dividend for me. Houston played the Dodgers in the World Series. Brent called me and said, "Hey, I have tickets, do you want to go?" I think you can guess my answer. What a great experience that was. I had mixed emotions when the Astros won the Series. I'm a longtime Dodgers fan, but I was excited for Brent.

Ron: Talk to me about how this type of training has evolved, because we're not doing the same things we did 15 years ago.

Jim: Back then we were really big on getting the body at certain positions through the delivery, and hitting the mark. But as it's evolved, that became less important. Now the mark is just something along the process. What we try to do now is build athleticism in the pitcher. Think of the pitchers of yesteryear, Bob Gibson, Sandy Koufax, even Nolan Ryan. These guys didn't just focus on getting their leg up high or getting their arm to a position. They were very athletic. They did things that were much more explosive for their time.

I think a reason so many pitchers have been on the disabled list over the last five years is because they baby their arms. We have an advanced class that's 90 minutes long, and we're not throwing until about an hour into that class. We're going to make sure we get all our throwing work in. But we're not going to worry so much about where the glove side is, where the arm is. We still want to hit certain marks, but we're not teaching that as an absolute. I think the totality of the delivery is much more important.

That's something that's evolved quite a bit over the years. I don't think someone wants to just stand there with their leg up in the air and hold their balance through the shin, or land and their glove stays in front. It's become more athletic, particularly in the last five or six years. In the beginning, we didn't emphasize athleticism. Now we do. Our pitchers have gotten better because we didn't teach them how to pitch, we taught them to be athletic and explosive and do things to train for explosiveness. And it's made all the difference in the world.

Ron: This has had a significant impact on the baseball universe at large.

Jim: Very much. I mentioned the Cleveland-Houston series. Those are two organizations you've had a huge impact on, from arm care to arm health. Particularly Cleveland, with Trevor and the things he's brought to the table like the Shoulder Tube, which was the brainchild of Robert Oates in terms of a conditioning tool. Trevor took to that like a fish to water. He even has his own clothing line that has the Shoulder Tube as part of the insignia.

Before games, you see two-pound weighted ball throws being made against the wall. You see different warmup routines. Weighted ball and velocity are important to the Dodgers. I mentioned Brent Strom. Derek Johnson, the pitching coach for Cincinnati, has been with you since he was the pitching coach at Stetson. So it's throughout baseball.

We're always changing and adapting at our facility. You just introduced a new piece of equipment that we hadn't gotten into yet, but we utilized it at the camp this week, and now guys are starting to use it at our facility. It's not to say we don't put our own spin on some of the things you do, but we know if it's been done at The Ranch, we definitely want to bring it to our table.

Recently I was talking to someone from the Angels organization. He said they've seen that the kids who are coming up are all doing some form of training, whether it's ours or other modalities. He said, "We have to get on board because these kids are training this way. We can't just take it away from them."

Ron: As people reading this already know, Brent and Derek are both in this book. What do you see for the future of this type of training? How big can it get? How impressive can the results be?

Jim: I think one thing we're going to find when players get older is some really big changes in the recovery after a player throws. That's another area baseball didn't really focus on. They would say, "Put a bag of ice on. And then you should be fine."

But over the last few years, we started adding things like the mock throw. We use a device called a mobility wrap. It's like a big rubber band. It's also known as Voodoo Floss. We're utilizing that in post-arm care and recovery. We're doing things like cupping, which is kind of an old Eastern "medicine" way of trying to help speed up recover. So I think recovery is going to become really big. We spend a lot of time on what happens after someone throws, to help build them back up.

We're also going to see a lot more in areas like mental wellbeing and nutrition. I believe guys are going to have a better understanding of how important nutrition can play in building a player's strength. I was talking to someone in the bodybuilding world, who said, "You have to eat a certain way if you're stressing the muscle, and you have to eat a certain way to build that muscle back up." That's no different in the pitching world, especially with the recovery of a shoulder, elbow, and such.

Then from a throwing standpoint, I think we're going to see guys doing routines that are going to take 30 to 45 minutes of warmup before they go out into a game. The game-day routine for the pitchers at my high school is a stretch routine with a dynamic warmup, with arm care, and then long toss. They spend an hour, including bullpen, before they step out on the mound. Our goal is to make sure these kids are prepared to throw.

I think that's where we're going with training. Kids will be spending the time doing a lot more than just do a couple arm circles and throw. I think we're going to start to see younger players start to understand this a little bit more. We're going to see a lot more preparation before a game, and a lot more time spent after a game to help recovery so the player can come back and be effective for the next game.

There are still a lot of old-school guys coaching kids. They don't think they need to learn new things because they played the game, even if that was 20 years ago. But if they were open to learning, they'd get so much from the continuing education your clinics and camps provide. It's so refreshing to see guys like Brent Strom, Derek Johnson, and Dave Lawn, the pitching coach at the University of Arizona, taking notes at these clinics. These guys are at the top of their profession. I joke that I wouldn't want to see my local competitors taking part in your clinics, but the fact is, it's just good for everyone to learn new things, and a better way of doing things.

Ron: As a high school coach, you deal with parents of athletes. As a parent, you raised a son who was an elite athlete. So what would you say to a parent who is thinking about taking their son to the Texas Baseball Ranch?

Jim: Whenever parents have asked me about it, I've always encouraged them to go. I've told them it would be the best investment they ever make. And every single one of them comes back and says, "Thank you, thank you, thank you. That was the greatest weekend. That was the greatest summer." I've had at least a dozen kids go there.

I think parents respect what I do. I've known in town as the pitching guy and the arm health guy. So if I tell somebody I think there's a benefit to something, they listen to me. That includes our camps here. Maybe traveling to Texas isn't an option for them. Recently a mom came to me to ask about our Elite Pitchers Boot Camp. I told her it would be the best weekend they'd ever had. When she asked me the price, and I told her, she nearly passed out. But she said, "Okay. I'm going to trust you on this." Then last weekend during the camp, I walked up to her and her husband and said, "So what do you think?" They said, "Oh my God. If you had charged us double, we still would've thought this was the best thing ever."

I think a benefit to parents of pitchers trying to find the best thing for their son is that I've gone through it as a parent. Like so many kids, my son's dream was to make the Major Leagues. He didn't make it to the pros, but he played Division I baseball. Most kids don't get that far. I always tell people his mom and I don't have one ounce of college debt because of it. Baseball paid his way. So I've lived through it. I've gone through the ups and downs. I've had to make emotional and financial decisions. This is part of what I can offer people. And I think they appreciate that foresight into what they might expect.

Ron: Final question: With any successful movement, you're going to have the copycats. You're going to have the mimics. You're going to have those that are going to try to imitate or replicate what's being done. The training systems we've implemented are the result of a lot of research and experience and specialized knowledge. Copycats won't have that. What would you say to a parent who's deciding where to take their son?

Jim: It starts with their workout. Will their son just get warmed up and then start throwing, or is there a plan in place to help him warm up to throw?

Number two is the drills they're doing. Is it static? Meaning, are they just trying to get you to lift your leg up? Are they just trying to teach you to point the ball back to second base? There are numerous studies that show reasons why pointing the ball back to second base is an injury waiting to happen. A lot of people don't know that because they don't investigate. They just say, "Oh, well so-and-so does it, so it must be fine."

I honestly believe parents will weed out the copycats after a few sessions. We actually get a lot of those parents coming to us. A number of coaches only work with students part-time. There are a few like that in my area. They do it after their regular job, so they see kids in the evening. But after a long day at work, they might just cancel on the kids. So those parents come to us and say things like, "He was working with a guy, but it wasn't very consistent. And he didn't seem to be growing much." They want growth, and they want consistency.

They also don't want their son to get hurt, which happens all too often without proper training and proper handling. That's why arm health is such an important part of what I do.

I'm not going to trash the other guys. I don't want parents thinking they messed up. I'll just say, "I know him, he's a good guy," and then move on from there. "Here's what we're going to do. I think you're going to really like this." The copycats aren't going to present themselves in that way. I think people see the difference, and I think that's part of what's made us so successful. There's a reason I'm still doing this after 17 years.

It's been a great ride so far, and it's far from over. It's constantly evolving and it's constantly changing. We've had some very good players come through our facility. Many have made it to professional baseball. So far Trevor is our only Major Leaguer, but I see us getting even better players in the future.

I have the best job in the world.

Ron: I can't argue with that. I'll just add, you're very good at this job. Jim Wagner, founder of Throwzone Academy, thank you for sharing your insights on velocity and arm health.

To Contact Jim Wagner:
Phone: 661.644.8814
Email: throwzone20@gmail.com
Website: www.Throwzone.com

EXTRA

INNINGS

FINAL THOUGHTS FROM COACH RON WOLFORTH

Wow! In my opinion, that was pretty darn neat! I will tell you it sure was fun catching up with these guys.

For me personally, reading or listening to a top thinker, influencer or practical applicator in our field is always a treat. It is my hope that being able to hear from ten of them in one central location, this book, was especially impactful for you.

I feel very fortunate to know all of these men well and have them as personal friends. Each of them has, in his own way, served as my teacher and has influenced and helped shape my philosophy, and in return has impacted hundreds, if not thousands, of young men that we have been privileged to work with at the Texas Baseball Ranch®.

I also view each of these men as partners and teammates in our 30+ year quest to investigate this mystery we refer to as 'pitching' and 'pitcher development'. I have a tremendous amount of respect and admiration for each of them, and Jill and I are so thankful for their support and cooperation for this project.

After reading this collection of interviews, I find there remains a series of follow-up questions for each reader of this book to ponder. For example:

1. So what? Why and in what specific ways were these interviews important and/or impactful to me or my personal situation?

2. How have these interviews changed me or shaped me? Have they primarily been reinforcement of what I already believe to be true, emboldening me to feel more confident in my current path or have they challenged my long-held beliefs and philosophies in some way and I need to sort some things out for myself?

3. Now what, what's next? Where do I go from here? What can I take and use from these interviews? Based on the information in these interviews, what do I need to further research or investigate?

As I alluded to in my introduction, my primary purpose in collecting and sharing the perspectives of today's top coaches and trainers was to give other coaches, instructors, trainers, parents and players a glimpse into the minds of some of baseball's premier pitching development thought leaders so they may gain, implement and/or pass it along to others.

Success leaves clues. The top 10% of performers in almost every field of endeavor always seem to behave and think differently than do the other 90%. These 10 men certainly behave and think differently.

Over my 60+ years of life, the universal truth that there is an incredibly important distinction to be made between knowledge and wisdom has never been more poignant to me than it is today.

I routinely remind my family, friends, staff and athletes that knowledge is only potential power. True, lasting change only occurs when that knowledge is practically applied, and its results are measured. My constant refrain serves as far more than simply sharing good advice to others. Most importantly, my prompt to others serves as a stark reminder to myself that the goal is in getting it right and not in impressing others with how smart one is.

Unfortunately, I know dozens of otherwise wonderful coaches, trainers and instructors who are very well versed in impressive baseball dogma and/or training jargon but fall far short in the areas of motor skill development and the transfer of training to game time performance.

In other words, on the surface many people may initially sound very accomplished and progressive but instead, under further review, are significantly lacking in depth and adroitness. There is of course a big difference between philosophy, terminology, specialized language, idiom, and verbal cueing compared to actually enhancing someone's mechanical efficiency and/or game time performance.

One thing is for certain, truly effective, master teachers are always quite rare and are absolutely worth their weight in gold, many times over. It was a real honor bringing you interviews from, in my opinion, 10 such master teachers.

From here the reader can proceed in several different ways:
If you are a coach, trainer or instructor:

- Come and visit us at the Ranch and observe first-hand how our coaching staff evaluates and trains athletes at an *Elite Pitchers Boot Camp* or our *Extended Stay Summer Development Program*. **There is never a fee for coaches to visit and observe**. Take all the notes you want. We just don't allow videotaping. We'd love to have you visit. Hundreds of coaches and trainers have visited the Ranch over the years, and we have built strong, wonderful lasting relationships with many of them.

- I would highly recommend attending the annual *Ultimate Pitching Coaches Bootcamp* (www.coachesbootcamp.com) held the first full weekend in December at the Texas Baseball Ranch®. There you will regularly hear presentations from these influencers and many, many others similar to them. In short, if you liked the book, you'll absolutely love the event.

- Become a member of the Coaches Durathro™ Monthly Inner Circle where you get digital access to the processes and protocols the Ranch uses on a daily basis plus a monthly newsletter, audio CD and bi-monthly vlog. (For more information, email info@texasbaseballranch.com)

- Purchase instructional training manuals & DVDs developed by the Texas Baseball Ranch® specific to your exact needs and interests to help supplement and lead your motor skill development processes, such as **Velocity Enhancement, Command Enhancement, Lower Half Utilization, Synergy and Coordination, Recovery and Next Generation Arm Care.**

- Take the concepts that are articulated in this book and begin to study them independently making your own conclusions and drawing your own inferences and distinctions.

If you are a parent or grandparent:

- We'd love to have you come and visit us at the Ranch. We'll give you a tour of the facility, introduce you to the staff and maybe, if the timing is right, you can observe the staff training athletes at an *Elite Pitchers Boot Camp* or our *Extended Stay Summer Development Program* and see if what you observe would benefit your son or grandson. We'd be honored to answer your questions and share with you our philosophies and methodology. Visit www.texasbaseballranch.com for more information or to request a free informational DVD and packet.

- Take the concepts that are articulated in this book and begin to study them independently making your own conclusions and drawing your own inferences and distinctions.

If you are a player:

- Come and visit us at the Ranch. We'll give you a tour of the facility, introduce you to the staff and maybe, if the timing is right, you can observe the staff training athletes at an *Elite Pitchers Boot Camp* or our *Extended Stay Summer Development Program*. Visit www.texasbaseballranch.com for more information or to request a free informational DVD and packet.

- Purchase instructional training manuals & DVDs developed by the Texas Baseball Ranch® specific to your exact needs and interests to help supplement and lead your motor skill development processes, such as **Velocity Enhancement, Command Enhancement, Lower Half Utilization, Synergy and Coordination, Recovery and Next Generation Arm Care.**

- Take what you learned in this book and begin to study these ideas and processes independently, making your own conclusions and drawing your own inferences and distinctions.

Until we meet in person, stay curious and keep fighting the good fight.

Welcome to the revolution.

Welcome to the Arms Race!

Texas Baseball Ranch:
Phone: 936-588-6762
Email: info@texasbaseballranch.com
Website: www.texasbaseballranch.com

WANT TO
PUBLISH A BOOK
LIKE THIS?

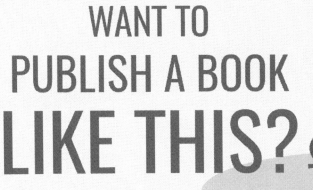

BMD PUBLISHING HAS PUBLISHED DOZENS OF BOOKS LIKE THIS IN NUMEROUS BUSINESS SECTORS.

OUR PROCESS IS EFFICIENT AND EFFECTIVE.

IF YOU'VE ALWAYS WANTED TO DO A BOOK BUT DIDN'T KNOW WHERE TO BEGIN, GO TO WWW.MARKETDOMINATIONLLC.COM/BMDPUBLISHING TO SET UP A **FREE** *TURN THE PAGE* CONSULTATION.

BEGIN AN EXCITING NEW CHAPTER IN YOUR LIFE!

IT'S YOUR TIME TO BECOME
AN AUTHOR

Made in the USA
Columbia, SC
06 August 2024

39672872R00111